AF662423

Senses 2

A Course in Environmental Science

Name: ....

Grade: .... Section: ....

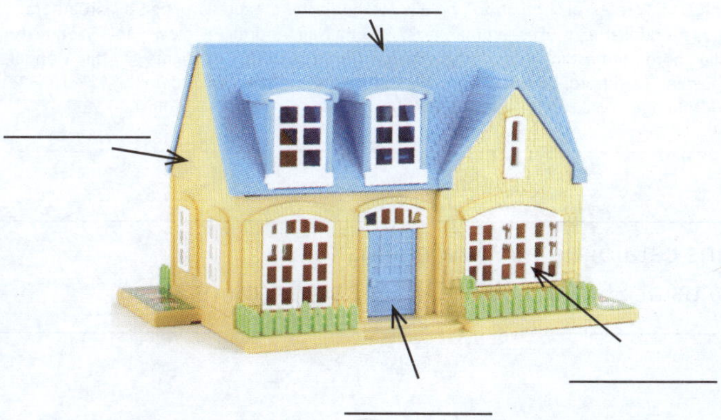

We live in a house. A house provides us shelter and safety. It protects us from heat, cold, rain, thieves, wild animals, dirt and dust.

Label the parts of a house.

Editor: Satyasree Gupta

HarperCollins*Publishers*

Publishing operations in 17 countries and 120+ imprints globally

William Collins' dream of knowledge for all began with the publication of his first book in 1819. A self-educated mill worker, he not only enriched millions of lives, but also founded a flourishing publishing house. Today, staying true to this spirit, Collins books are packed with inspiration, innovation and practical expertise. They place you at the centre of a world of possibility and give you exactly what you need to explore it.

Published by Collins Learning
An imprint of HarperCollins*Publishers* India
Building No. 10, Tower A, 4th Floor, DLF Cyber City, Gurugram, Haryana 122002, India

First edition: 2024
Reprint edition: 2025
ISBN: 978-93-6213-238-3

Artwork and typesetting by SeedBox6
Layout by Pallavi Kapur
Content created by ExcelSoft Technologies Pvt. Ltd.
Printed and bound in India by MicroPrints India, New Delhi

ACKNOWLEDGEMENTS

Inside: pg 2: pijama61, pg 3: Artis777, pg 4: KanKhem, muhammad, sofyan, hadi, Natalie_, eliflamra, pg 7: Jose A. Bernat Bacete, Dimitris66, CollinsChin, dageldog, carlosalvarez, pg 8: eliflamra, pa 18: R-DESIGN, Lew Robertson, lasdairJames, Vlad Fishman, kaanates, pg 11: jayk7, AshaSathees Photography, fcafotodigital, Francesco Carta fotografo, David Burton, wilatlak villette, Maren Caruso, Natasha Breen, AlasdairJames, kaanates, RedHelga, AlasdairJames, pg 12pg 12: Ivan, lacaosa, EyeWolf, Lew Robertson, pg 16: PandaVector, pg 18: IconicBestiary, Bakhauaddin-bek Sopybekov, pg 19: Designer_things, graphic-bee, zuperia, msonick, David Malan, Elena Abramovich, pg 20: colematt, blueringmedia, pg 21: wilatlak villette, Henrik5000, Maria Rytova, IconicBestiary, Suraj Raheja, Val_Iva, artpartner-images, Eric Schaeffer, pg 23: Nadya Ustyuzhantseva, pg 25: mariaflaya, sarunyu_foto, yotto, fotiksonya, Good Job, pg 26: VIDOK, sarayut Thaneerat, phototropic, ATU Images, kaisphoto, wilatlak villette, pg 27: 7romawka7, ithinksky, Charles O'Rear, hanh Bui, pg 28: ©Daniela White Images, pg 29: negatina, Fernando Trabanco Fotografía, Chris Griffiths, ziss, Jonathan R. Beckerman, firemanYU, Andrey Sayfutdinov, T&I studio, R.Tsubin, pg 32: KanKhem, Catherine Falls Commercial, Betsie Van der, Meer, pg 34: Anton Petrus, MarcelTB, Aditya Singh, Mike Hill, Rebecca R Jackrel, James Warwick, Nancybelle Gonzaga Villarroya, wildestanimal, Alan Tunnicliffe Photography, pg 35: Laura Hedien, James Warwick, Volanthevist, MediaProduction, Jose A. Bernat Bacete, pg 36: wera Rodsawang, Alan Shapiro, Jyoti Sangya, Michael Roberts, Robbie Goodall, Burazin, Darrell Gulin, pg 37: KanKhem, Hennadii, Hennadii, Joe McDonald, pg 38: mark hughes, "Ale-ks", Hailshadow, pg 39: Life On White, Michael Duva, rusm, Alexander W Helin, SandroSalomon, Michael Duva, Nongbassbasic, Juan Silva, macroworld, pg 41: Juan Silva, pg 44: Blanchi Costela, Barcin, nyvltart, ayvengo, pg 45: eliflamra, solar22, pg 46: Pokota Poco, CoolFinger, cgdeaw, klyaksun, Colorfuel Studio, cgdeaw, Tetiana Lazunova, pg 48: Peter Dazeley, pg 49: jattumongkhon, pg 51: lutavia, pg 53: jiraporn Meereewee, bortonia, pg 60: bgblue, pg 61: axstokes, pg 62: zhengjie wu, sarayut Thaneerat, wilatlak villette, R.Tsubin, simonkr, pg 63: David Crespo, nevio3, Geraint Rowland Photography, sbayram, pg 64: smartboy10, miava, erhui1979, CSA-Printstock, pg 67: yelet, pg 68: Carlos Fernandez, pg 70pg 70: Christophe Lehenaff, ectortatu, pg 71: Christophe Lehenaff, inhauscreative, Space Frontiers, pg 72: amtitus, Magnilion, shomos uddin, pg 75: Andrew Aitchison, viktor_vector, ose A. Bernat Bacete, pg 76: annedala,Nayanba Jadeja, pg 77: kbeis, pg 78: uniquely india, IndiaPix/IndiaPicture, VW Pics, Lane Oatey/Blue Jean Images, tdub303, AVEENDRAN / Staff, REDA&CO / Contributor, oonal, triloks, pg 79: triloks, SnowWhiteimages, NurPhoto / Contributor, Pgiam, IndiaPix/IndiaPicture, AFP / Stringer, triloks, David Clapp, Liyao Xie, danishkhan, fordzolo, pg 80: mikroman6, Grace Cary, Poh Kim Yeoh / EyeEm, jayk7, jayk7, Leonid Sneg, enter89, RoyalFive, Kyryl Gorlov, Xsandra, Manuel Breva Colmeiro, pg 87: Aslan Alphan, Joe Schmelzer, LordRunar, pg 88: Tuul & Bruno Morandi, Alan Powdrill, Ganesh Bastola, THEPALMER, pg 89:, 89: NurPhoto, Adam Crowley, Medesulda, Education Images, Bike_Maverick, RUSSELLTATEdotCOM, PATSTOCK, pg 90: robuart, Toltemara, exxorian, pg 91: Vyacheslav Argenberg, Oleh_Slobodeniuk, Buena Vista Images, pg 96: dodo4466, appleuzr, Si-Gal, filo, Designer, RUSSELLTATEdotCOM, "professorphotoshop", pg 97: doodlemachine, scotellaro, pg 98: FatCamera, pg 99: Poodle Soup, Onoontour, Pavlo Plakhotia, pg 106: BDphoto, Sanjay Borra, subodhsathe, mukesh-kumar, jayk7, Veena Nair, Andrea Pistolesi, PaoloGaetano, Dinodia Photo, My image, George Pachantouris, Fanatic Studio, pg 107: Dinodia Photo, Hindustan Times, ImagesBazaar, Dinodia Photo, Copyrights @ Arijit Mondal, NurPhoto, shigemitsu, IndiaPix/IndiaPicture, NurPhoto, Bambam Kumar Jha / EyeEm, NurPhoto, Dinodia Photo, pg 108: daz2d, pg 114: cenkerdem, pg 115: New York Daily News Archive, pg 116: alexsl, Bakhauaddin-bek Sopybekov, pg 117: PM Images, Maksim Prasolenko, BRO Vector, mrs, pg 120: Riou, Colorfuel Studio

Browse the complete Collins catalogue at www.collins.in.
For any queries/feedback, please write to us at SCHOOLSUPPORT@harpercollins.co.in.

Preface

Senses is an environmental science series for **grades 1 to 5** that strictly adheres to the National Curriculum Framework 2023 (NCF 2023). The series helps students understand concepts, patterns, processes (social and natural) and interconnections between the environment and human society. The series uses interactive pedagogical techniques to help students gain a more systematic understanding of their environment and its impact on human life.

The series incorporates all the guidelines of the latest NCF. The themes and topics of the series are mapped to the Curriculum goals and Competencies as outlined in the NCF 2023. Every chapter starts with the list of Curriculum goals and corresponding competencies as mapped in the chapter.

The content is structured to enable students to observe, understand, analyse and describe the process of interdependence between the natural environment and society. Various activities and creative do-it-yourself projects help the students expand their observation and apply what they have learnt to the real world.

Several tasks and activities mindfully interspersed in each chapter encourage students to interact with the concepts and process and in turn apply relevant learning skills such as creative thinking, critical thinking, problem-solving skills and life skills to understand the world around them.

A separate segment on the United Nations Sustainable Development Goals (SDGs) connects the students with various critical global issues like pollution, global warming, etc., and ensures that they stay informed and reflect on how they can make the world a better place to live.

The cross-curricular activities take care of the interdisciplinary approach and ensure that students develop a holistic view of the world. The detailed assessments ensure that the core competencies are gained and learning outcomes have been achieved.

Senses is our attempt to ensure that students are sensitive towards the environment and that they respect diversity and work towards preservation of the environment.

About the author

Satyasree Gupta is the editor of the grades 1 and 2. She has an in-depth understanding of pedagogy and the different curricula prevalent in India. She has authored several books, and mentored hundreds of educators across the globe. She holds a dual PhD in Education Management and Doctorate in Science.

Learning and Development During the Foundational Stage

The Foundational Stage is a single curricular and pedagogical phase comprising five years of flexible, Development During multilevel, play and activity-based learning for children the Foundational Stage during these years must focus on developing foundational years as critical to development and learning. Education between 3 and 8 years of age. NEP 2020 sees these early capacities and skills: cognitive, linguistic, and socio emotional. In fact, this period is the most sensitive for socio-emotional development. In addition to these skills, education during this period should help children to develop good learning habits. Together, the skills developed during this Stage form the bedrock for children to learn academic reading and writing and numeracy as they mature as well as provide a foundation for lifelong learning.

Various branches of study including developmental biology, psychology and cognitive neurosciences have helped us understand the different aspects of development that must be emphasized at this stage to achieve the desired goals. These are also captured in the panchakosha description in the *Taittiriya Upanishad*, which is one of the earliest descriptions of the different domains of development of the human being. These domains are:

Physical Development, or *annamaya* kosha and *pranamaya* kosha understood together, includes bodily awareness and embodies learning through active engagement of all sensorial perceptions. Reflected in basic things like jumping to challenging tasks like writing, proper physical development at this stage enables children to grow into fit and healthy adults. Children require a multitude of opportunities for meaningful learning experience that support physical development through play and guided activities.

Special Features: Creators Corner, Let's Start, Try It

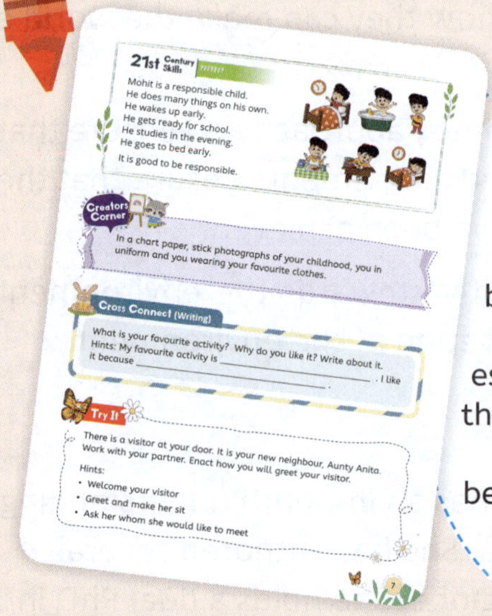

Socio-emotional and Ethical Development:

Emotional and spiritual development or the *manomaya* kosha involves becoming aware of and skilfully regulating our emotions. It is during this stage that children become aware of their emotions, other people and the world around them. Hence, experiences during this stage help to establish and mould many facets that will eventually make up the personality of the adult. This makes it necessary for children to have adequate opportunities to explore, understand and become aware of their own emotions, preferences and reactions to situations and people.

Special Features: 21st Century Skills, Cross Connect

Cognitive Development:
This refers to the development of the intellect, or *vijnanamaya* kosha, which means to engage meaningfully with the cognitive and conscious aspects of human experience. Puzzles and riddles have been traditionally used to support cognitive development. Sometimes, children need more support in the form of experiences, thought-provoking questions, and basic problem solving. Identifying patterns, relationships between objects, thinking logically—these are key skills in present times.
Special Features: Try It, Engage and Reflect, Different Yet Alike, HOTS

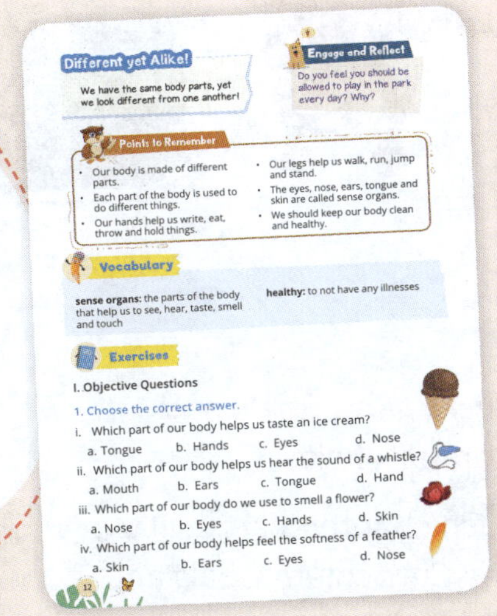
Different yet Alike!
We have the same body parts, yet we look different from one another!
Engage and Reflect
Do you feel you should be allowed to play in the park every day? Why?
Points to Remember
- Our body is made of different parts.
- Each part of the body is used to do different things.
- Our hands help us write, eat, throw and hold things.
- Our legs help us walk, run, jump and stand.
- The eyes, nose, ears, tongue and skin are called sense organs.
- We should keep our body clean and healthy.

Vocabulary
sense organs: the parts of the body that help us to see, hear, taste, smell and touch
healthy: to not have any illnesses

Exercises
I. Objective Questions
1. Choose the correct answer.
i. Which part of our body helps us taste an ice cream?
a. Tongue b. Hands c. Eyes d. Nose
ii. Which part of our body helps us hear the sound of a whistle?
a. Mouth b. Ears c. Tongue d. Hand
iii. Which part of our body do we use to smell a flower?
a. Nose b. Eyes c. Hands d. Skin
iv. Which part of our body helps feel the softness of a feather?
a. Skin b. Ears c. Eyes d. Nose

12

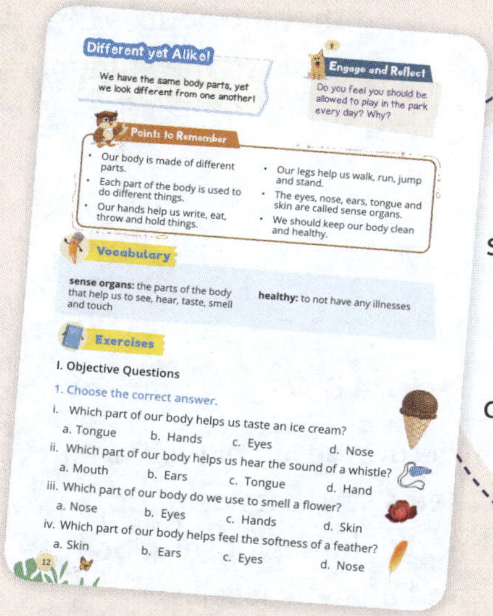
Different yet Alike!
We have the same body parts, yet we look different from one another!
Engage and Reflect
Do you feel you should be allowed to play in the park every day? Why?
Points to Remember
- Our body is made of different parts.
- Each part of the body is used to do different things.
- Our hands help us write, eat, throw and hold things.
- Our legs help us walk, run, jump and stand.
- The eyes, nose, ears, tongue and skin are called sense organs.
- We should keep our body clean and healthy.

Vocabulary
sense organs: the parts of the body that help us to see, hear, taste, smell and touch
healthy: to not have any illnesses

Exercises
I. Objective Questions
1. Choose the correct answer.
i. Which part of our body helps us taste an ice cream?
a. Tongue b. Hands c. Eyes d. Nose
ii. Which part of our body helps us hear the sound of a whistle?
a. Mouth b. Ears c. Tongue d. Hand
iii. Which part of our body do we use to smell a flower?
a. Nose b. Eyes c. Hands d. Skin
iv. Which part of our body helps feel the softness of a feather?
a. Skin b. Ears c. Eyes d. Nose

12

Language and Literacy Development:
Language development goes beyond reading and writing. It also includes the ability to communicate clearly and comprehend what children hear and read. While listening and speaking skills are developed through routine activities, it takes concerted effort to develop the skills of reading and writing. With the current NEP emphasis on Foundational Literacy, it is imperative to provide children with a print-rich environment along with multiple learning opportunities to acquire and hone their skills in various languages.
Special Features: Vocabulary, Engage and Reflect, end-of-chapter questions

Aesthetic and Cultural Development:
Anandamaya kosha, or experience of transcendence, is best addressed for this age group through arts and culture. The importance of the arts and culture in shaping the personality of children cannot be overemphasized. Children need opportunities to experience the arts for themselves so that they can learn to appreciate it.
Special Features: Chapter 15:

15 Celebrations

Curricular Goals	Competencies
CG-4 Children develop emotional intelligence, i.e., the ability to understand and manage their own emotions, and responds positively to social norms CG-7 Children make sense of world around through observation and logical thinking	C-4.1 Starts recognising 'self' as an individual belonging to a family and community C-7.1 Observes and understands different categories of objects and relationships between them

Let's Start
Make a Diwali or a Christmas greeting card.
To whom would you like to give this card? Tell us why.

Finally, it is during this stage that children acquire habits that help them become lifelong learners. At the end of this stage, children move to more formal learning environments. Hence, these habits equip them with the skills they need to learn and grow in school and continue through their life.

Key Features

Curriculum Goals and Competencies

Each chapter starts with the Curriculum Goals and Competencies to be covered in the chapter.

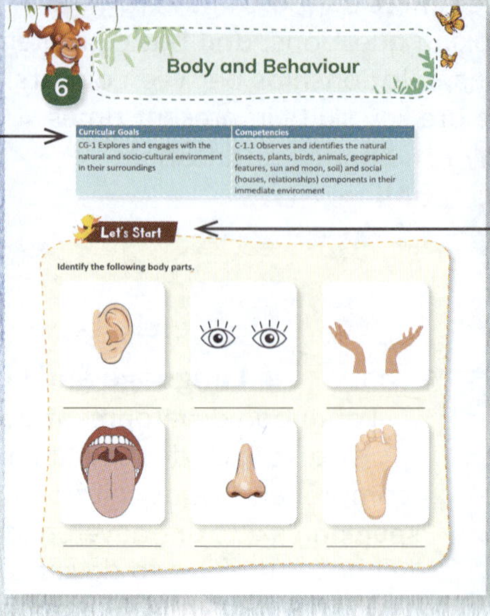
6

Body and Behaviour

Curricular Goals	Competencies
CG-1 Explores and engages with the natural and socio-cultural environment in their surroundings	C-1.1 Observes and identifies the natural (insects, plants, birds, animals, geographical features, sun and moon, soil) and social (houses, relationships) components in their immediate environment

Let's Start

Identify the following body parts.

Let's Start!

Warm-up activity that introduces the topic to the students

Engage and Reflect

An experiential learning activity which encourages students to engage with the environment and reflect on his/her observations

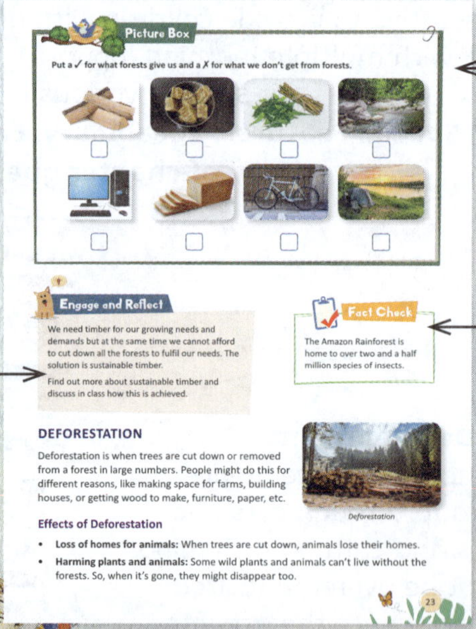
Picture Box

Put a ✓ for what forests give us and a ✗ for what we don't get from forests.

Engage and Reflect

We need timber for our growing needs and demands but at the same time we cannot afford to cut down all the forests to fulfil our needs. The solution is sustainable timber.

Find out more about sustainable timber and discuss in class how this is achieved.

Fact Check

The Amazon Rainforest is home to over two and a half million species of insects.

DEFORESTATION

Deforestation is when trees are cut down or removed from a forest in large numbers. People might do this for different reasons, like making space for farms, building houses, or getting wood to make, furniture, paper, etc.

Deforestation

Effects of Deforestation

- **Loss of homes for animals:** When trees are cut down, animals lose their homes.
- **Harming plants and animals:** Some wild plants and animals can't live without the forests. So, when it's gone, they might disappear too.

23

Picture Box

Picture-based activity that helps students develop and enhance observation and analytical skills

Fact Check

Lists interesting facts related to the chapter

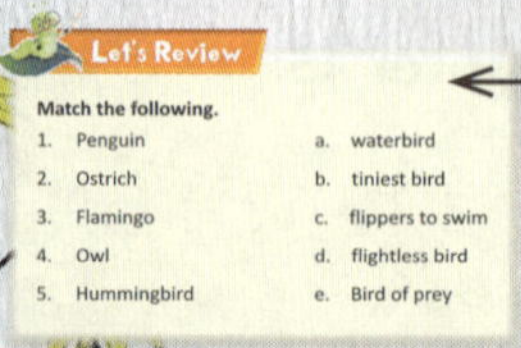
Let's Review

Match the following.

1.	Penguin	a.	waterbird
2.	Ostrich	b.	tiniest bird
3.	Flamingo	c.	flippers to swim
4.	Owl	d.	flightless bird
5.	Hummingbird	e.	Bird of prey

Let's Review

In-text activities to help revise the concepts learnt

SDG Connect

An info-activity based on application of **Sustainable Development Goals**

SDG Goals

Natural heritage refers to plants, landforms, waterbodies, forests and animals. The SDG 11.4 wants us to *work towards protecting and safeguarding the world's natural heritage*. Find out the natural heritage of your state. What will you do to protect the natural heritage of your state?

21st Century Skills — Information Literacy

With the advent of summer, the use of air conditioners increases. Air conditioners are harmful for our environment. Find out what other methods can be adopted to keep our homes/offices/school cool without the use of air conditioners.

21st Century Skills

Activities based on the 21st century skills

Points to Remember

Snippets of information for quick recapitulation

Cross Connect

Interdisciplinary activities interconnecting topics from different subjects that make the learning more holistic

Try It

Helps students apply the concepts learnt in the real world

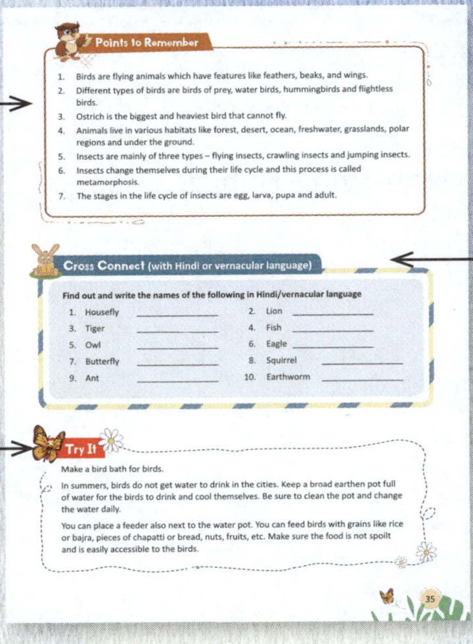
Points to Remember

1. Birds are flying animals which have features like feathers, beaks, and wings.
2. Different types of birds are birds of prey, water birds, hummingbirds and flightless birds.
3. Ostrich is the biggest and heaviest bird that cannot fly.
4. Animals live in various habitats like forest, desert, ocean, freshwater, grasslands, polar regions and under the ground.
5. Insects are mainly of three types – flying insects, crawling insects and jumping insects.
6. Insects change themselves during their life cycle and this process is called metamorphosis.
7. The stages in the life cycle of insects are egg, larva, pupa and adult.

Cross Connect (with Hindi or vernacular language)

Find out and write the names of the following in Hindi/vernacular language

1. Housefly	______	2. Lion	______
3. Tiger	______	4. Fish	______
5. Owl	______	6. Eagle	______
7. Butterfly	______	8. Squirrel	______
9. Ant	______	10. Earthworm	______

Try It

Make a bird bath for birds.

In summers, birds do not get water to drink in the cities. Keep a broad earthen pot full of water for the birds to drink and cool themselves. Be sure to clean the pot and change the water daily.

You can place a feeder also next to the water pot. You can feed birds with grains like rice or bajra, pieces of chapatti or bread, nuts, fruits, etc. Make sure the food is not spoilt and is easily accessible to the birds.

35

Creators Corner

Provides space for the students for creative activities related to the topic

Creators Corner

Leaf Art

You can make leaf art using fallen and yellowed leaves. See the image below for a few examples. You can use your imagination and make some other interesting figures too. So look around, collect fallen leaves and enjoy!

Exercises

Competency-based assessment at the end of each chapter

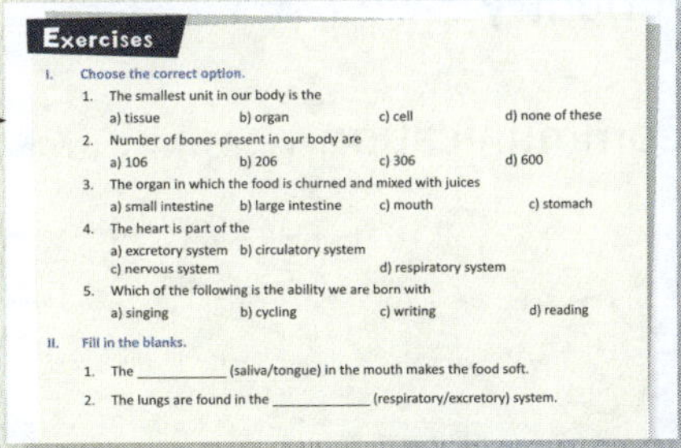
Exercises

I. Choose the correct option.

1. The smallest unit in our body is the
   a) tissue b) organ c) cell d) none of these
2. Number of bones present in our body are
   a) 106 b) 206 c) 306 d) 600
3. The organ in which the food is churned and mixed with juices
   a) small intestine b) large intestine c) mouth c) stomach
4. The heart is part of the
   a) excretory system b) circulatory system
   c) nervous system d) respiratory system
5. Which of the following is the ability we are born with
   a) singing b) cycling c) writing d) reading

II. Fill in the blanks.

1. The ____________ (saliva/tongue) in the mouth makes the food soft.
2. The lungs are found in the ____________ (respiratory/excretory) system.

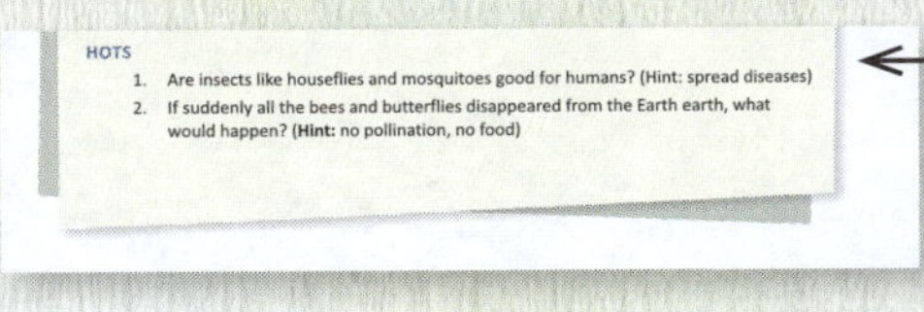
HOTS

1. Are insects like houseflies and mosquitoes good for humans? (Hint: spread diseases)
2. If suddenly all the bees and butterflies disappeared from the Earth earth, what would happen? (**Hint:** no pollination, no food)

HOTS

Questions and activities related to higher order thinking skills

Contents

1. I am Bigger 1
2. My Food 9
3. Living Things and Non-living Things 17
4. Plants 24
5. Animals 33
6. Air 42
7. Water 51
8. The Earth 60
9. The Sky 68
10. Clothes We Wear 76
11. Houses 86
12. My Neighbourhood 95
13. India—My Country 104
14. Modes of Communication 112

1 I am Bigger

Curricular Goals	Competencies
CG-4 Children develop emotional intelligence, i.e., the ability to understand and manage their own emotions, and responds positively to social norms	C-4.1 Starts recognising 'self' as an individual belonging to a family and community

Let's Start

Draw some patterns on the clothes. You can also colour the clothes using your favourite colours.

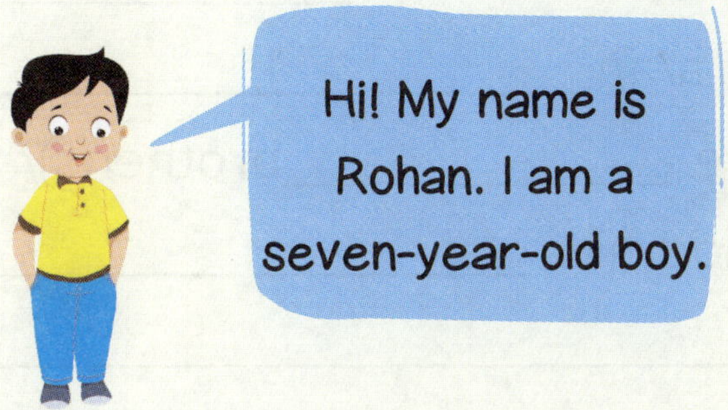

Let me tell you about myself.

I study in class 2. I live in Bengaluru with my parents. My address is:

House No. 7041, Brigade View, Ramachandrapura Road, Malleshwaram, Bengaluru – 560003

An **address** is information about where someone lives.

Now introduce yourself!

My name is ______________________________.

I am ______________ years old.

My mother's name is ______________________________.

She is a/an ______________________________.

My father's name is ______________________________.

He is a/an ______________________________.

I have ____________brother(s)/____________sister (s)/no sibling.

My address: ______________________________

____

My parents' phone numbers are ______________________________.

Never share your name, address or phone number with unknown people.

I am bigger

I was born as a baby. I had no teeth then.

I was not able to do many things on my own.

Now I have grown up into a boy.

I can do many things on my own.

We grow bigger each year.

Many changes happen as we grow:

- We become taller.
- We grow stronger.
- Our old clothes and shoes do not fit us.

A young boy grows up into a man.

A young girl grows up into a woman.

Things I can do on my own

I can **spell** and write my name.

I can write the names of my family members too.

Fact Check

Our body stops growing after some years, but our hair and nails grow throughout our life.

I can read a book.

I can make my bed.

I can comb my hair.

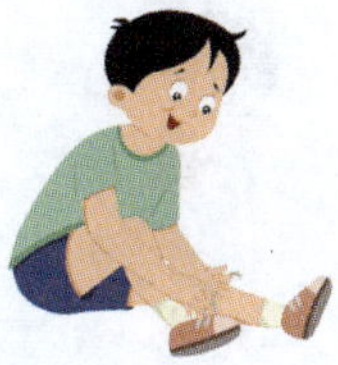

I can tie my shoelaces.

I can ride a bicycle.

Likes and Dislikes

Everyone has likes and dislikes.

Like is some thing that make us happy and we enjoy doing.

I like dancing.

I like swimming.

I like watching cartoons.

What do you like to do? I like to ______________________________.

Dislike is something that do not make us happy and that we do not enjoy doing.

I dislike bursting crackers.

What do you dislike?

I dislike

_____________________.

Engage and Reflect

Rohan likes watching cartoon shows. Her parents do not allow her to watch cartoons for more than 30 minutes every day.
Is it good to watch cartoons for long hours? Why?

Hobbies

Everybody likes to do some activities in their free time. A hobby is an activity that we do in our free time. Hobbies help us relax. They make us happy.

People have different hobbies. Drawing, dancing, reading, singing and gardening are some of the common hobbies.

Drawing

Dancing

Reading

Singing

Gardening

I like painting. My friend, Anita, likes cycling.

What is your hobby? My hobby is ______________________________.

Points to Remember

- We introduce ourselves to someone by telling them our name.
- We become taller and stronger as we grow.
- We can do many things on our own as we grow.
- Everyone has likes and dislikes.
- Hobbies are the activities that we like to do in our free time.

Vocabulary

spell: write or name the letters that form a word

like: be fond of

dislike: not like

Exercises

I. Objective Questions

1. Tick (✓) the correct answer.

i. What are we all born as?

a. Babies b. Men c. Women d. Girls

ii. What does a baby boy grow up into?

a. Baby b. Man c. Woman d. Girl

iii. What does a baby girl grow up into?

a. Baby b. Man c. Woman d. Girl

iv. Which of the following can be someone's hobby?

a. Fighting b. Shouting c. Crying d. Reading

v. Which of the following will not change when you grow up?

a. Your height b. Your eyes c. Your clothes d. Your shoes

2. Fill in the blanks using the words given in the box.

Many	name	hobbies	taller	address

i. An ________________ is information about where someone lives.

ii. ____________________ changes happen as we grow.

iii. We become _____________________ as we grow.

iv. Everyone has a __________.

v. The activities we do in our free time are called __________.

3. Write T for True and F for False.

i. We can share our mobile number and address with an unknown person. ☐

ii. A newborn baby has teeth. ☐

iii. Everyone has their likes and dislikes. ☐

iv. I cannot do anything on my own. ☐

v. I am stronger now compared to when I was born. ☐

II. Subjective Questions

1. What is an address?

An address is ____.

2. List some of your hobbies.

Some of my hobbies are ____

____.

3. List five activities that you can do on your own.

I can ______________. I can ______________. I can ______________.

I can ______________. I can ______________.

4. List three changes that you have gone through since you were a baby.

The three changes that I have undergone since I was a baby are:

____

____.

III.HOTS

1. **Identify if Anil is a baby/man/woman after reading the clues given below.**

   no teeth, less hair on the head, cannot sit or stand, crawls around the house

   Anil is a ________________________________.

2. **Look at the table showing the likes and dislikes of Mohan, Tina and Payal. Then answer the following questions.**

	 Juice	 Carrots	 Dogs	 Cycling	 Green colour
Mohan	✓	✗	✓	✓	✗
Tina	✗	✓	✗	✓	✓
Payal	✓	✓	✗	✓	✗

i. What does Mohan like? ______________________________

ii. Who likes cycling? __________________________________

iii. What does Payal dislike? _____________________________

iv. What are the things liked by both Mohan and Payal? __________
____

v. What are the things that both Tina and Payal dislike? __________
____

21st Century Skills — Life skills and values

Suhana is a 7-year-old girl. She completes all her work on time. She wakes up early in the morning, she bathes, dresses herself, eats breakfast and goes to school on time. Suhana has learnt to manage her time well.

We should do our things on time.

Creators Corner

Make your scrapbook.

Make a five page booklet. Decorate the cover page. Write the following on each page.

Name: Birthday: Phone number:

Your favourite:

- colour
- game
- cartoon show
- food
- book
- hobby

Get it filled by five friends.

Cross Connect (Writing)

We feel happy doing the activities we like. Write about the activities that make you happy and sad.

i. I am happy when ______________________________.

ii. I am sad when ______________________________.

Try It

Ask your parents to show you the picture of you as a baby. Compare it with the way you look now. What changes do you see?

2 My Food

Curricular Goals	Competencies
CG-1 Children develop habits that keep them healthy and safe	C-4.1 Starts recognising 'self' as an individual belonging to a family and community
CG-7 Children make sense of world around through observation and logical thinking	C-7.1 Observes and understands different categories of objects and relationships between them C-7.2 Observes and understands cause and effect relationships in nature by forming simple hypothesis and uses observations to explain their hypothesis

Let's Start

Vegetable printing

Cut a lady's finger and an onion in half. Dip the lady's finger into the blue paint and the onion into the orange paint. Using these to create a pattern below.

Let us learn about food.

Why do we eat food?

We need food to live. It gives us **energy**. It keeps us healthy and helps us grow. We get food from different sources.

Sources of Food

We get food from both plants and animals.

Radish

Carrot

Food from plants

We get fruits and vegetables from plants. They contain **nutrients** that help our bodies stay fit and healthy.

Different fruits and vegetables have different nutrients. We should eat all types of fruits and vegetables. All fruits are eaten **raw**. Most vegetables are cooked before eating. Some vegetables like carrots and radish can be eaten raw.

We also get pulses and cereals from plants. Pulses and cereals are seeds that are eaten. Cereals include wheat, rice, maize, oats, millets, etc. Pulses include kidney beans, chickpeas, black gram, green lentils, etc. These come in different shapes and colours.

Nuts like almonds, cashews, walnuts, peanuts are also food items that we get from plants.

Kidney beans

Chickpeas

Cashews

Walnuts

We get oil from seeds, fruits and nuts. We use oil to cook food. Which cooking oil is used in your home?

Food from animals

We get milk, eggs, meat, fish and honey from animals.

We get milk from cows, buffaloes and goats. We can make curd, butter and cheese from milk.

Milk is considered as a complete food because it has many important nutrients.

Different yet Alike!

We get different types of oils from different plants.

We get mustard oil from mustard seeds, coconut oil from coconut and olive oil from the olive fruit.

Mustard oil

Coconut oil

Olive oil

Milk

Eggs

Meat

Curd

Butter and Cheese

Types of Food

There are different types of food. Each type of food helps us in different ways. We should eat all kinds of food. Our food is mainly divided into three groups: Energy-giving food, Body-building food and Protective food.

Energy-giving food

Food that gives us energy to work and play is called energy-giving food. A few examples of energy-giving food are wheat, rice, potato, bread, and sugar. We should include energy-giving foods in all our meals.

Rice

Wheat

Bread

Potato

Sugar

Body-building food

Food that helps us to grow and make our bones and muscles stronger is called body-building food. A few examples of body-building food are milk, eggs, dal, chicken, fish and soya.

Milk

Soya chunks

Chicken

Fish

Eggs

Protective food

Food that protects our bodies from diseases and illnesses is called protective food. A few examples are fruits and vegetables.

Fruits and Vegetables

Eating Healthy

We should follow healthy food habits to stay fit. Some of the healthy eating habits are:

- We should eat a balanced meal. A meal that has the right amount of energy-giving, body-building and protective food is called a **balanced meal.**
- We should drink enough water every day. We should drink clean water.
- We should always wash our hands properly before and after eating food.
- We should wash vegetables and fruits properly before eating them. This removes the germs and the dirt.
- We should eat fresh food. Food should always be kept covered. We should not eat uncovered food.

- We should chew our food properly.
- We should include more fruits and vegetables in our meals.

Picture Box

Tick (✓) the good practices and cross out (✗) the bad practices.

i. 

ii. 

iii. 

Engage and Reflect

Is it good to eat only your favourite food for all the meals in a day? Think.

Points to Remember

- The food that we eat comes from plants and animals.
- Energy-giving food, body-building food and protective food are different types of food.
- The food that gives us energy to work and play is called energy-giving food. Examples: wheat, rice, sugar
- The food that helps us grow is called body-building food. Examples: milk, eggs, fish
- The food that protects us from diseases and illness is called protective food. Examples: fruits, vegetables
- We should follow healthy eating habits.

Vocabulary

energy: the strength to do different things

nutrients: found in food that help us live and grow

raw: food that is not cooked

balanced meal: meal that includes food from all groups

Exercises

I. Objective Questions

1. Tick (✓) the correct answer.

i. Identify the INCORRECT sentence.

a. Food is a source of energy.

b. Food protects us from diseases and illnesses.

c. Food comes from animals and plants.

d. We can live without food for a long time.

ii. Which of the following is made from an animal product?

a. Curd b. Rice c. Roti d. Dal

iii. Identify the odd one out.

a. Orange b. Banana c. Apple d. Milk

iv. Which of the following is a healthy eating habit?

a. Not washing hands before having food

b. Eating a variety of food

c. Not drinking enough water

d. Eating only your favourite food every day

v. Which is a body-building food?

a. Eggs b. Potatoes c. Sugar d. Rice

2. Fill in the blanks using the words given in the box.

plants	balanced	Food	grow	animals

i. ____________________ gives us energy to work.

ii. A ____________________ diet includes food from all groups.

iii. We get food from ____________________ and animals.

iv. Eggs, milk and meat come from ____________________.

v. Body-building food helps us to ____________________.

3. Write T for True and F for False.

i. We should eat outside food regularly. ☐

ii. We should wash our hands before eating food. ☐

iii. We should only eat fruits and vegetables every day. ☐

iv. We should swallow our food without chewing. ☐

v. We should drink enough water every day. ☐

II. Subjective Questions

1. Why do we need food?

____

2. What are the different plant products that we eat?

____

3. Why should we eat different kinds of food?

____

4. Write any two healthy eating habits.

____

III. HOTS

1. Nowyou know the importance of different kinds of food. Can you plan your school lunch for a day? What will you include and why?

____

2. Make a list of food items that you have brought for your lunch today. Has anyone brought the same food? Give reasons.

____

21st Century Skills | Life skills and values

Misri's mother gives her something healthy to munch in between meals. Misri has also learnt to make a fruit salad. She is fond of other snacks such as nuts, sprouts and oat-jaggery laddus. You should also munch on healthy snacks like Misri and avoid junk food.

We should eat healthy food.

Creators Corner

Collect pictures of different dishes from different parts of India. Draw a map of India on a chart paper and paste the pictures in the correct place on it.

Cross Connect (Writing)

Name your favourite food. Find out how it is prepared.

My favourite food is______________________________

Try It

Make a snack at home without using fire and treat your family. You can use biscuits, bread, ketchup, jam, etc.

3 Living Things and Non-living Things

Curricular Goals	Competencies
CG-7 Children make sense of world around through observation and logical thinking	C-7.1 Observes and understands different categories of objects and relationships between them C-7.2 Observes and understands cause and effect relationships in nature by forming simple hypothesis and uses observations to explain their hypothesis

Let's Start

Complete and colour.

Complete the following drawings and colour them. Use green colour for the object that can move on its own and red colour for the object that cannot move on its own.

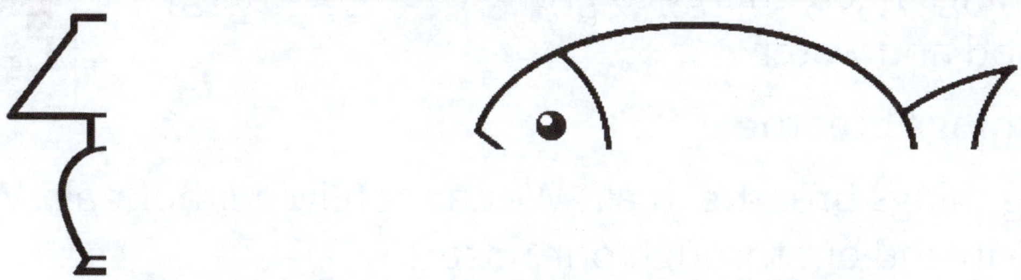

Let us learn about living things and non-living things.

We see a lot of things around us like cars, animals, stones, buildings, trees, people and so on. These things can be grouped into living things and non-living things.

Things that breathe, eat, grow, move on their own and give birth to young ones are called **living things.** All plants and animals are living things.

Engage and Reflect

Are there street dogs in your neighbourhood? Does your family care for them? Why or why not?

Things that do not breathe, eat, grow, move on their own are called **non-living things.** Mountains, water, vehicles and toys are non-living things.

Features of living things

Living things move

Living things can move from one place to another on their own. Animals move from one place to another in search of food and **shelter**. We move from one place to another with our legs.

Plants cannot move. They make their own food using sunlight, water and soil.

Living things eat

Living things need energy to grow. They get energy from food and water.

Living things breathe

All living things **breathe** in air. We cannot live without air. We breathe in and out through our nose.

Place your hand under your nose. Do you feel the air going in and out?

Living things grow

All livings things grow and become big.

A plant grows into a tree.

A baby grows into an adult.

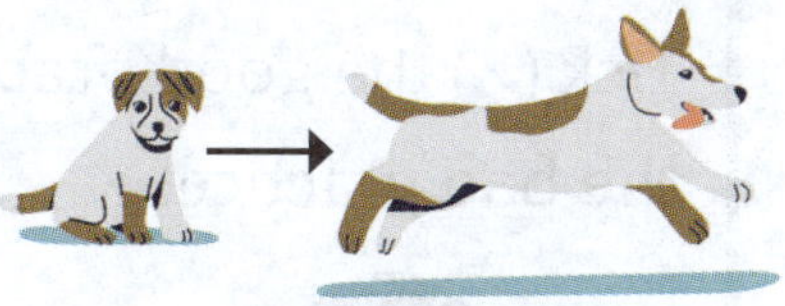

A puppy grows into a dog.

Living things give birth

All living things give birth to young ones of their own kind.

Humans give birth to babies. Some animals such as monkeys, cats, cows and elephants give birth to young ones.

Some animals such as crocodiles, snakes and birds lay eggs. Their young ones hatch from the eggs.

Features of non-living things

Non-living things are different from living things.

Non-living things:

- do not move on their own.
- do not eat.
- do not breathe.
- do not grow.
- do not give birth to young ones.

Different yet Alike!

The work done by living things are being replaced by non-living things. Nowadays, we have robots that clean the house and voice search that can talk to us.

We cannot live without some of the non-living things such as air, water and sunlight. Other examples of non-living things are chair, toys, table, pencil, books, bag, house, car, aeroplane and ship.

Picture Box

Tick (✓) the good practice and cross (✗) the bad practice.

i.

ii.

iii.

Fact Check

Do you think that all things that move or grow are called living things? Look up on a cloudy day. You will observe that the clouds are moving and growing but they are non-living things. The river also moves (flows), but is it a living thing?

Points to Remember

- Living things move, eat, breathe, grow and give birth to young ones.
- Non-living things do not move, eat, breathe, grow or give birth to young ones.

Vocabulary

features: qualities

breathe: take air inside and let it out

shelter: a place to protect oneself from the surroundings and danger

Exercises

I. Objective Questions

1. Tick (✓) the correct answer.

i. Identify the non-living thing(s).

a. 

b. 

c. 

d. 

ii. Which of the following is not a feature of a living thing?

a. Can grow b. Can eat c. Cannot sleep d. Can move

iii. A ________ is a non-living thing.

a. Plant b. Baby c. Pencil d. Cat

iv. Identify the non-living thing in the sentence.
In Ramesh's house, there is one big car and one small puppy.

a. big car b. puppy c. Ramesh d. none of the above

v. Tick (✓) the odd one out.

a. 

b. 

c. 

d. 

2. Fill in the blanks using the words in the box.

Animals	air	Living	non-living	grow

i. ________________ things can give birth to young ones.

ii. ________________ move from one place to another in search of food and shelter.

iii. Living things need energy to _______________.

iv. All living things need _______________ to breathe.

v. Cars, buses, computers, stones, buildings etc., are _______________ things.

3. Write T for True and F for False.

i. A paper boat floating in water is a living thing. [ ]

ii. A forest has many living things. [ ]

iii. All living things need air to breathe. [ ]

iv. A kitten is a living thing as it grows into a cat. [ ]

v. A kite is a living thing as it flies in the air. [ ]

II. Subjective Questions

1. List the features of living things.

____

2. Name two living things and two non-living things.

____

3. Plants do not move but are still called living things. Give reasons.

____

4. How are non-living things different from living things?

____

III. HOTS

1. Name five non-living things that can move.

____

2. Are a toy kitten and a real kitten the same? How are they different?

____

21st Century Skills | Life skills and values

Ayesha saw a wounded puppy while returning home from the playground. She took help from an adult to take the puppy home. She helped her parents to apply the medicine on its wound.

She also likes to take care of plants. She helps her parents in the garden.

We should be sensitive and caring towards other living things.

Creators Corner

Complete the following seed art. Recreate the image given here on a chart paper.

Paste yellow gram in the petals of the flowers, and mustard seeds in the centre of the flowers. Colour the stems green with a crayon. Use any gram/seed of your favourite colour for the vase.

Cross Connect (Writing)

Describe the most beautiful thing you have seen. Is it a living thing or a non-living thing?

Try It

Visit a park. Make a list of the different living things and non-living things around you.

4 Plants

Curricular Goals	Competencies
CG-4 Children develop emotional intelligence, i.e., the ability to understand and manage their own emotions, and responds positively to social norms Children develop a positive regard for the natural environment around them	C-4.6 Shows kindness and helpfulness to others (including animals, plants) when they are in need
CG-6 Children develop a positive regard for the natural environment around them	C-6.1 Shows care for and joy in engaging with all life forms
CG-7 Children make sense of world around through observation and logical thinking	C-7.2 Observes and understands cause and effect relationships in nature by forming simple hypothesis and uses observations to explain their hypothesis

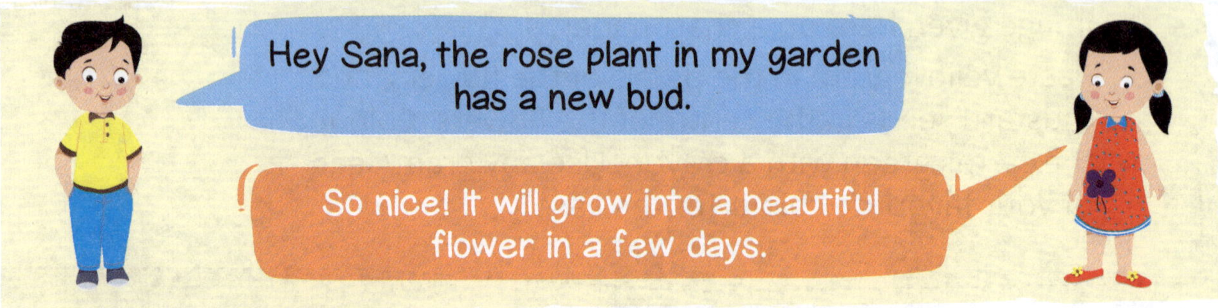

Let's Start

Leaf painting

Collect fallen leaves of different shapes and sizes. Take one leaf. Paint one side of the leaf with your favourite colour. Carefully, place the leaf, painted side down, in the given box. Press on the leaf for a few seconds. Remove the leaf. Do the same with other leaves. Your leaves painting is ready.

Let us learn about plants.

We can see plants all around us. They give us fresh air, food, wood and many more things. They are important living things.

Parts of a plant

There are six main parts of a plant. Let us learn about each part.

Roots

Roots are the part of the plant that grows below the soil. The roots hold the plant **firmly** to the ground. They absorbs water and **nutrients** from the soil. The roots are usually brown in colour.

Parts of a plant

Stem

The stem is the part of the plant that grows above the ground. It connects the root to other parts of the plant. It bears branches, leaves, flowers and fruits.

Leaves

Leaves prepare food for the plants with the help of sunlight, air, water and nutrients from the soil. They are called the kitchen of the plant. Leaves are mostly green in colour. Some leaves are broad, some are small and some are narrow and long.

Banana

Rose

Bamboo

Pine

Flowers

Flowers are the beautiful and colourful parts of the plants. All flowers look different and smell different. Some of the flowers are rose, lotus, sunflower and hibiscus.

Rose

Lotus

Sunflower

Hibiscus

Fruits

The fruit protects the seeds. We eat the fruits of the plant. Some of the fruits are apples, mangoes and watermelons.

Seeds

Seeds are the hard part present inside a fruit. Some seeds are tasty. They are good for our health. New plants grow from seeds.

Different yet Alike!

Plants have flowers of different colours. Roses come in many colours: red, white, pink, yellow and white.

Which colour rose do you like most?

____

Engage and Reflect

Plant some kidney beans and some black grams in two different pots with the help of your parents. Observe the pots for about a week.

Which plant grew first? ______________

Types of plants

Plants are all around us. Some are big and some small.

Trees

Trees are big, tall and strong plants. They have a hard, thick and brown stem called a trunk. They have many branches. These branches have leaves, flowers and fruits. Trees have deep, long and strong roots. They can live for many years. Neem, oak, jackfruit, banyan and coconut are some examples of trees.

Neem tree

Shrubs

Shrubs are smaller than trees. They have thin, brown and woody stems. They have many branches. Tulsi, pomegranate, rose, lemon are some of the examples of shrubs.

Tulsi plant

Herbs

Coriander

Engage and Reflect

Trees are cut for many reasons—to build roads, to get wood for making furniture, etc, and so on. Is this right? Do we need to do anything to reduce the cutting down of trees?

Herbs are small plants with thin, green and soft stems. Some of the herbs are used as medicines. Coriander, spinach, rice and mustard are some examples of herbs.

Climbers

Climbers are plants with weak stems that need support to stand. They climb on other plants, sticks or walls to grow. Grapevine, pea, bean, and cucumber are some examples of climbers.

Grapevine

Creepers

Creepers have very weak stems and thin branches. They grow along the ground. Most creepers have big fruits. Pumpkin, strawberry and watermelon are examples of creepers.

Pumpkin

Picture Box

Tick (✓) the good practice and cross (✗) the bad practice.

i. 

ii. 

iii. 

Fact Check

The touch-me-not plant is a creeper that closes its leaves when someone touches it.

Points to Remember

- Roots, stem, leaves, flowers, fruits and seeds are the main parts of a plant.
- Trees are big plants with strong stems.
- Shrubs are small plants with strong stems.
- Herbs are small plants with soft stems.
- Climbers are plants with weak stems that need support to stand.
- Creepers are plants with very weak stems that grow along the ground.

Vocabulary

firmly: strongly

support: hold

protect: guard

nutrient: materials found in soil that help plants to grow

trunk: hard, thick and brown stem of a tree

Exercises

I. Objective Questions

1. Tick (✓) the correct answer.

i. Which of the following is a tree?

a.  b.  c.  d. 

ii. Which of the following describes a climber?

a. It has a weak stem. c. It has green leaves.

b. It needs support to climb. d. All the above

iii. Which of the following is a feature of a grapevine?

a. Hard stem b. Thick stem c. Woody stem d. Weak stem

iv. Which of the following is a herb?

a.  b.  c.  d. 

v. Which of the following makes food for the plant?

a.  b.  c.  d. 

2. Fill in the blanks using the words in the box.

Stem	Rose	Trunk	Money	Herb

i. ________________ plant is an example of a shrub.

ii. ________________ plant is an example of a climber.

iii. ________________ is the hard, thick and brown stem of a tree.

iv. ________________ is the part of the plant that grows above the ground.

v. Spinach plant is an example of________________.

3. Write T for True and F for False.

i. Flowers are called the kitchen of the plant. ☐

ii. Herbs have strong stems. ☐

iii. Creepers grow along the ground. ☐

iv. Trees live only for some months. ☐

v. Plants give us fresh air to breathe. ☐

II. Subjective Questions

1. Draw a plant and label its different parts.

2. Name the different types of plants based on their growth.

3. Write two differences between a herb and a shrub.

4. List the functions of the stem in a plant.

III. HOTS

1. Razia wants to decorate her garden wall. Which type of plants should she grow?

2. Milkhan lives on the 7th floor of a building. He is planning to grow a garden on his balcony. Suggest the different types of plants that he can grow on his balcony.

   [Hint: Think of plants that can be planted in pots.]

21st Century Skills | Life skills and values

Nithya's family celebrates her birthday every year by planting as many saplings as her age. She turned seven this year, so they planted seven different saplings.

We should plant more trees for a better life.

Creators Corner

Collect different types of flowers from the garden. Do not pluck flowers. Pick the fallen ones. Dry and paste them into your scrapbook.

Cross Connect (Writing)

Write about your experience of planting and watching a plant grow.

____

____

____

Try It

Grow a potato plant in a pot or your garden. Do it with an adult.

First, wear gloves. Then make the soil ready by mixing a handful of manure in it.

Next, cut the buds from the potatoes and plant them.

Cover the potatoes with some soil and water them. After a few days, your potato plant will start growing. Keep watering them at regular intervals.

5

Animals

Curricular Goals	Competencies
CG-4 Children develop emotional intelligence, i.e., the ability to understand and manage their own emotions, and responds positively to social norms Children develop a positive regard for the natural environment around them CG-6 Children develop a positive regard for the natural environment around them CG-7 Children make sense of world around through observation and logical thinking	C-4.6 Shows kindness and helpfulness to others (including animals, plants) when they are in need C-6.1 Shows care for and joy in engaging with all life forms C-7.2 Observes and understands cause and effect relationships in nature by forming simple hypothesis and uses observations to explain their hypothesis

Let's Start

Warli art

In Warli art, simple shapes are used to draw animals and people. Draw the animal and bird in this art form as shown below. Name the animal and bird.

____

____

Let us learn about animals.

Food habits of animals

What do animals eat?

Like us, animals need food to live. Different animals eat different things such as leaves, fruits, grass, insects, and other animals. Animals are grouped according to the type of food that they eat.

Different yet Alike

Various animals eat their food in different ways. Snakes swallow, cows chew, dogs lap up, butterflies suck and squirrels bite their food.

- Animals that eat plants and plant products are called plant-eaters or **herbivores**. Cow, goat, horse, giraffe, rabbit, etc. are some examples of herbivores.

Cow

Horse

Rabbit

Goat

- Animals that eat insects, worms and the flesh of other animals are called flesh-eaters or **carnivores.** Lion, tiger, shark, wolf, polar bear, etc. are some examples of carnivores.

Polar bear

Lion

Tiger

Shark

These animals kill smaller animals for food. Such smaller animals are called their **prey.**

- There are animals that eat both plants and the flesh of other animals. These animals are called plant-and-flesh eaters or **omnivores**. Fox, bear, crow, gorillas, etc. are some examples of omnivores.

Bear

Gorillas

Fox

Based on the food that you eat, which group do you belong to? Herbivores, Carnivores or Omnivores?________________________

Birds

- Birds are animals that have wings. These wings help them fly.
- A few birds, like the ostrich and penguins cannot fly.

Ostrich

Penguin

- Birds have two legs that help them walk.

Engage and Reflect

Many animals perform at the circus. Some of these animals are captured from the forests, caged and trained to learn and perform tricks.

Do you think this is a good practice? Give a reason.

- Birds have feathers on their bodies. Feathers keep their body warm.
- A bird's mouth is called a beak. It is used for eating.

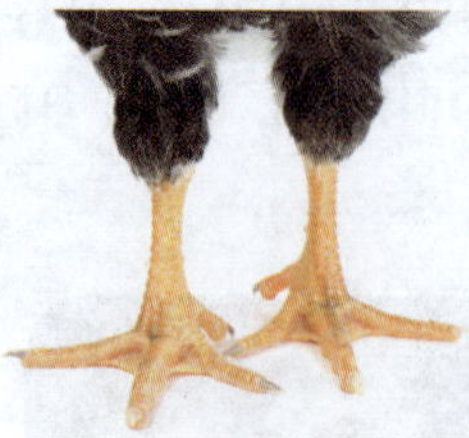
Feet

Feathers

Beak

What do birds eat?

Birds eat seeds, grains, fruits, insects and worms. A few birds like the vulture eat flesh.

A bird eating grains.

A bird eating fruits.

A bird eating insects.

Insects

Insects are very small creatures. Insects can be found everywhere.

Some insects have wings to fly. Some insects do not have wings. They hop about from one place to another.

Housefly

Beetle

Cockroach

Butterfly

Features of insects

- Insects have six legs.
- They have **antennae** on their head.

Body of an insect

What do insects eat?

- Most insects are plant-eaters. They eat leaves, roots, seeds, etc.
- Some insects eat other insects.
- Some insects suck the blood of other animals, birds and human being.

Fact Check

Chameleons can extend their tongue up to 1.5 times their body length to catch their prey.

Picture Box

Tick (✓) the good practices and cross (✗) the bad practices.

i.  ☐

ii.  ☐

iii. 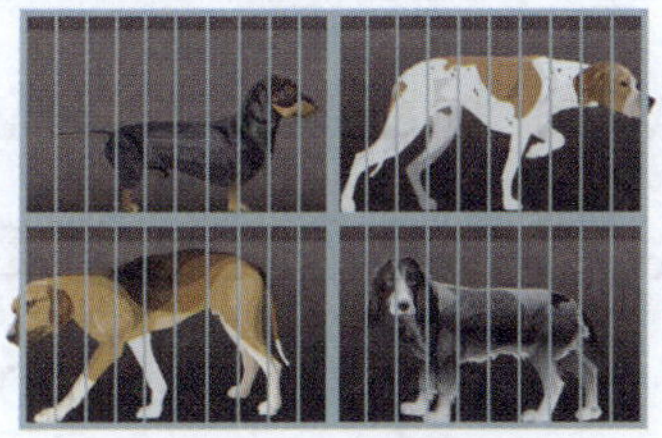 ☐

Points to Remember

- Herbivores are plant-eating animals such as cows, horses, goats, etc.
- Carnivores are flesh-eating animals such as lions, tigers, wolves, etc.
- Omnivores eat both plants and animals such as bears, crows, etc.
- Birds have wings, feathers and a beak.
- Birds eat seeds, grains, fruits, insects,worms and the flesh of other animals.
- Insects are small creatures with six legs.
- Insects eat plants or other insects. A few insects suck the blood of other animals or human being.

Vocabulary

prey: animal which is hunted by another animal for food

beak: hard pointed part of a bird's mouth

antenna: two long thin parts on an insect's head

Exercises

I. Objective Questions

1. Tick (✓) the correct answer.

i. Which of the following does a tiger eat?

a. Trees b. Grass c. Bananas d. Deer

ii. Which of the following eats only grass, leaves and fruits?

a. Carnivores b. Omnivores c. Herbivores d. None of the above

iii. Which is the odd one out?

a.  b.  c.  d. 

iv. Which of the following sentences is INCORRECT?

a. Birds have wings.

b. Birds eat grains, seeds and other insects.

c. Insects are herbivores.

d. Some insects have wings.

v. Which of the following is an omnivore?

a. Cow b. Giraffe c. Fox d. Leopard

2. Fill in the blanks by choosing the words from the box.

antennae	two	herbivores	six	wings	omnivores

i. Animals that eat plants are called ________________.

ii. Birds have ________________ that help them fly.

iii. Some insects have ________________ on their heads.

iv. Birds have ________________ legs and insects have ________________ legs.

v. Fox and bear are examples of ________________.

4. Match the animals to their food.

i. 		a. 
ii. 		b. 
iii. 		c. 
iv. 		d. 
v. 		e. 

II. Subjective Questions

1. What are herbivores? Give two examples.

____

____

2. What are omnivores? What do they eat?

____

____

3. Write one similarity between carnivore and omnivore.

____

____

4. Describe birds. What do birds eat?

____

____

III. HOTS

1. Mukund had a cow. His parents also got him a dog. Can he feed the animals the same food? Give a reason.

____

____

2. Shona, the rabbit, is very hungry. Help Shona find her favourite food by solving the maze.

21st Century Skills — Life skills and values

There are many stray dogs in Ojas's neighbourhood. One day he saw a dog getting hurt by a bicycle. Ojas was very sad. He asked his parents how he could help the stray dogs. His parents told him about the animal rescue homes in their city. Ojas called up the rescue home for help.

Help street animals.

Creators Corner

Discover a new animal by taking the features of two or more animals (for example, the tail of a squirrel, mane of a lion, wings of a bird, etc.). Draw it on a chart paper. What would you like to name it? What would the animal eat? Create three such animals.

Cross Connect (Writing)

If I were an animal, I would be a/an ______________________
because ____
____

Try It

Recreate the table on a chart paper. List two animals, two birds and two insects that you have seen in your neighbourhood. If you do not know their names, draw them. Observe the food they eat and complete the table.

Name of the Animal/Bird/Insect	Food they eat

6 Air

Curricular Goals	Competencies
CG-6 Children develop a positive regard for the natural environment around them	C-6.1 Shows care for and joy in engaging with all life forms
CG-7 Children make sense of world around through observation and logical thinking	C-7.2 Observes and understands cause and effect relationships in nature by forming simple hypothesis and uses observations to explain their hypothesis

Let's Start

Join and Colour

Join the numbers and colour it! What is the object called?

Fill in the missing letters.

W ___ N D ___ ___ L L

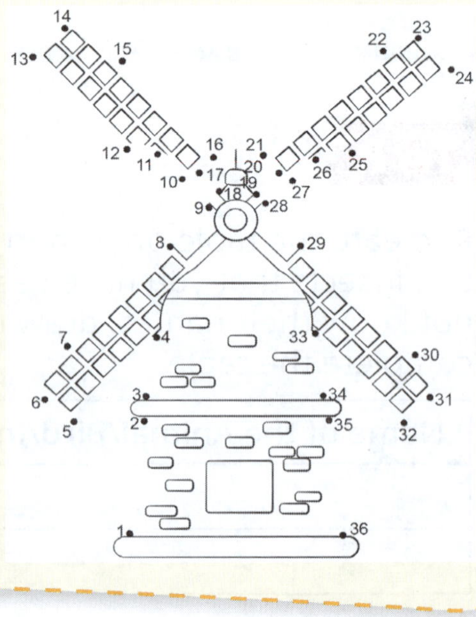

Let us learn about air.

Air is all around us. We need air to breathe. Animals and plants also need air to breathe. Plants need air to make their food.

Air has many properties. Let us learn about some of them.

Properties of air

Air cannot be seen.

We cannot see air, but we can feel it.

Can you feel the air when you stand in front of the fan?

Air occupies space.

Let us do an activity.

Take a balloon.

Blow air into it.

You will observe that the balloon becomes bigger when filled with air. This shows that air occupies space.

What do we do when our bicycle tyre goes flat? We fill the air in it.

Air has weight.

Take two similar balloons, a ruler and a thread.

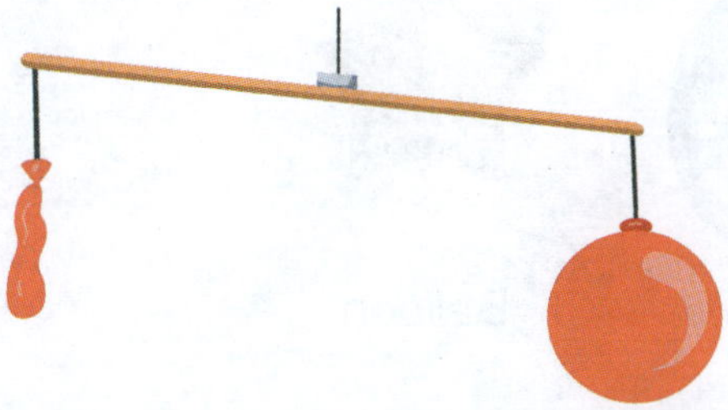

Tie the thread at the centre of the ruler to make a balance.

Blow one of the balloons. Tie the blown balloon at one end and the flatten balloon at the other end of the ruler using a thread as shown in the image.

Fact Check

Air moves in a particular direction. Windsocks are used at airports to indicate the direction of the wind to the pilots.

You will observe that the side with balloon with air goes down. This shows that the balloon with air is heavier than the balloon without air. Thus, we can say that air has weight.

Engage and Reflect

Take a candle and a glass container. Light the candle with the help of an adult. Now, cover the candle with the glass container. What did you observe?

The candle was put off. Do you know why?

Air helps in the burning of an object. Fire needs air.

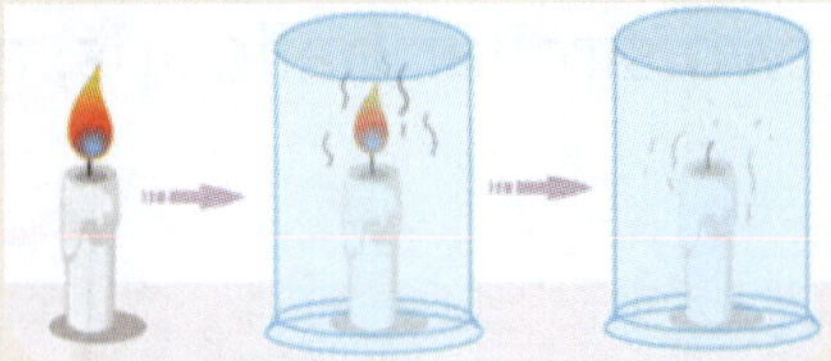

Air does not have a definite shape.

Air takes the shape of the object it is filled into.

Football

Tyre

Balloon

Air has no taste and no smell.

Pure air has no taste or smell. The smell of perfumes, food, flowers, and smoke are some smells that mix with air.

How to keep the air clean?

When you for a walk in the morning, how does the air feel?

Now think how does the air feel when you are near a traffic signal on a busy day?

The air is clear, clean and fresh in the park in the mornings, whereas the air is dirty and unclear near a traffic light.

Clean air is good for breathing. Plants keep our air clean.

Dust, smoke and other dirt particles make the air dirty. Smoke and fumes coming from the vehicles also make the air dirty. Dirty air looks **hazy** and brownish. It smells bad.

Dirty air due to smoke coming from vehicles

Air mixed with dust, dirt particles, smoke and fumes is called air pollution. This air is harmful to all living things. We may fall sick if we breathe this air.

Ways to keep the air clean

- Open windows in the morning to let fresh air in.
- Plant more trees in your area. Keep indoor plants. They improve the air inside the house.
- Avoid throwing garbage in the open. Always keep your dustbins covered.
- Walk or cycle wherever possible.
- Do not burn plastics.
- Do not burst firecrackers.

Engage and Reflect

Should we burst firecrackers? Why or why not?

Open windows and doors to let fresh air in.

Plant indoor plants. Plant trees to keep the air clean.

Burning plastics is bad for the air.

Bursting firecrackers causes air pollution.

Picture Box

Tick (✓) the good practice and cross (✗) the bad practice.

i. 

ii. 

iii. 

Points to Remember

- We cannot see air, but we can feel it.
- Air has weight.
- Air occupies space.
- Air does not have a shape.
- Air has no taste or smell.
- Dirty air is harmful to all living beings.
- We should keep the air clean.

Vocabulary

space: a place that is empty

fumes: smoke

hazy: not clear

ill: feeling unwell

disease: an illness that weakens the body

Exercises

I. Objective Questions

1. Tick (✓) the correct answer.

i. Which of the following is true about air?

a. Air has shape.
b. Air has taste.
c. Air has weight.
d. Air has smell.

ii. Two similar balloons are blown with the same amount of air. They are tied to either ends of a ruler. Which of the following will be true?

a. The ruler will bend towards the right.
b. The ruler will bend towards the left.
c. The ruler will remain straight.
d. The balloons will burst.

iii. Which of the following does not need air?

a. 
b. 
c. 
d. 

iv. Which of the following does not have a definite shape?

a. apple
b. bottle
c. chair
d. smoke

v. What does dirty air look like?

a. clear
b. clean
c. fresh
d. hazy and brownish

2. Fill in the blanks using the words given in the box.

space	air	football	clean	smoke

i. __________ air is important for good health.

ii. Air gets dirty with dust and _________.

iii. __________ is all around us.

iv. Air occupies __________.

v. A __________ is filled with air.

3. Write T for True and F for False.

i. A balloon filled with air is lighter than a balloon with no air. ☐

ii. An empty bottle has air inside it. ☐

iii. We should collect and burn all the garbage in the open. ☐

iv. Pooja is wearing perfume. You can smell it across the room. ☐

v. A flat tyre has no air in it. ☐

II. Subjective Questions

1. 'We cannot see air, but we can feel it'. Explain the sentence with an example.

____

____

2. List the properties of air.

____

____

3. Anees is packing his bags for a trip. He wants to pack his ball, swimming tube and sand toys. The swimming tube is too big to be packed in his bag. Can you suggest a way in which he can pack it?

____

____

4. What makes the air around us dirty?

____

____

III. HOTS

1. What happens when you suck air through a straw dipped inside a glass of fruit juice?

i. The straw blows up like a balloon due to the presence of air in it.

ii. The juice flows into your mouth through the straw.

iii. The juice comes out of the glass.

iv. Nothing happens.

2. "Air near the forests is cleaner than the air in the cities." Do you agree? Give reasons.

____

____

21st Century Skills | Life skills and values

While reading a newspaper, Liza read about the bad quality of air in her city. A few measures to keep the air clean were also given.

Liza went and asked her parents if they could follow the measures to keep the air clean. They chose to do the following things:

- Walk or cycle wherever possible.
- Use public transport to travel to her uncle's house.
- Her father started carpool to work.

Like Liza and her family, we should also do things that will help keep the air around us clean.

Creators Corner

Collect pictures from newspapers or magazines related to air pollution. Make a collage of it.

Cross Connect (Writing)

If you are granted a wish to have any one property of air,which one will you choose and why?

____

____

____

Try It

Do this activity with the help of your teacher or an adult.

Take a container filled with water. Take an empty bottle.

Invert the bottle and push it into the water in the container. What happens?

Now, tilt the bottle and push it into the water in the container. Share your observations.

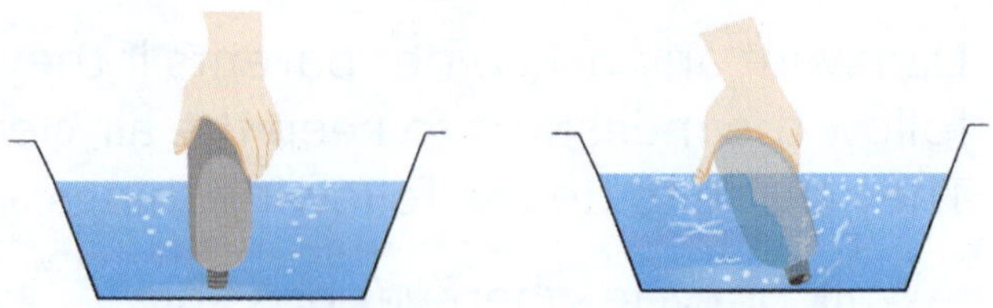

7 Water

Curricular Goals	Competencies
CG-6 Children develop a positive regard for the natural environment around them	C-6.1 Shows care for and joy in engaging with all life forms
CG-7 Children make sense of world around through observation and logical thinking	C-7.2 Observes and understands cause and effect relationships in nature by forming simple hypothesis and uses observations to explain their hypothesis

Let's Start

Blow Art

Take watercolours, mixing bowls, a dropper, a straw and a sheet of paper.

Mix different colours using water in different bowls. Place a drop of each on a sheet of paper using a dropper. Now, take the straw, place it on a drop of colour. Blow air into the straw from the other end. Similarly, blow on all the coloured drops. The coloured water droplets spread and form beautiful patterns.

Let us learn about water.

Water is important for all living things. We need water for drinking, bathing, cooking, washing, and many more activities. We cannot live without water.

Rain, underground water, rivers, seas and oceans are some of the sources of water.

Forms of water

Water exists in three forms. They are solid, liquid and gas.

Ice is the solid form of water.

Water is the liquid form of water.

Vapour is the gas form of water.

Water cycle

Different yet Alike!

Water, water vapour, ice, hail and snow are all different forms of water!

Do you know where clouds get water from?

When the sun heats the water in rivers, lakes and oceans, the water turns into **vapour**. This water vapour moves up into the air in the sky.

High up the air is cooler. The water vapour changes into water droplets. These water droplets form clouds. When the clouds become heavy, the water droplets fall back to the ground in the form of rain.

The rain may fall back into the oceans, lakes, rivers or land.

The continuous movement of water from land into the air and back to the land is called the **'water cycle'**.

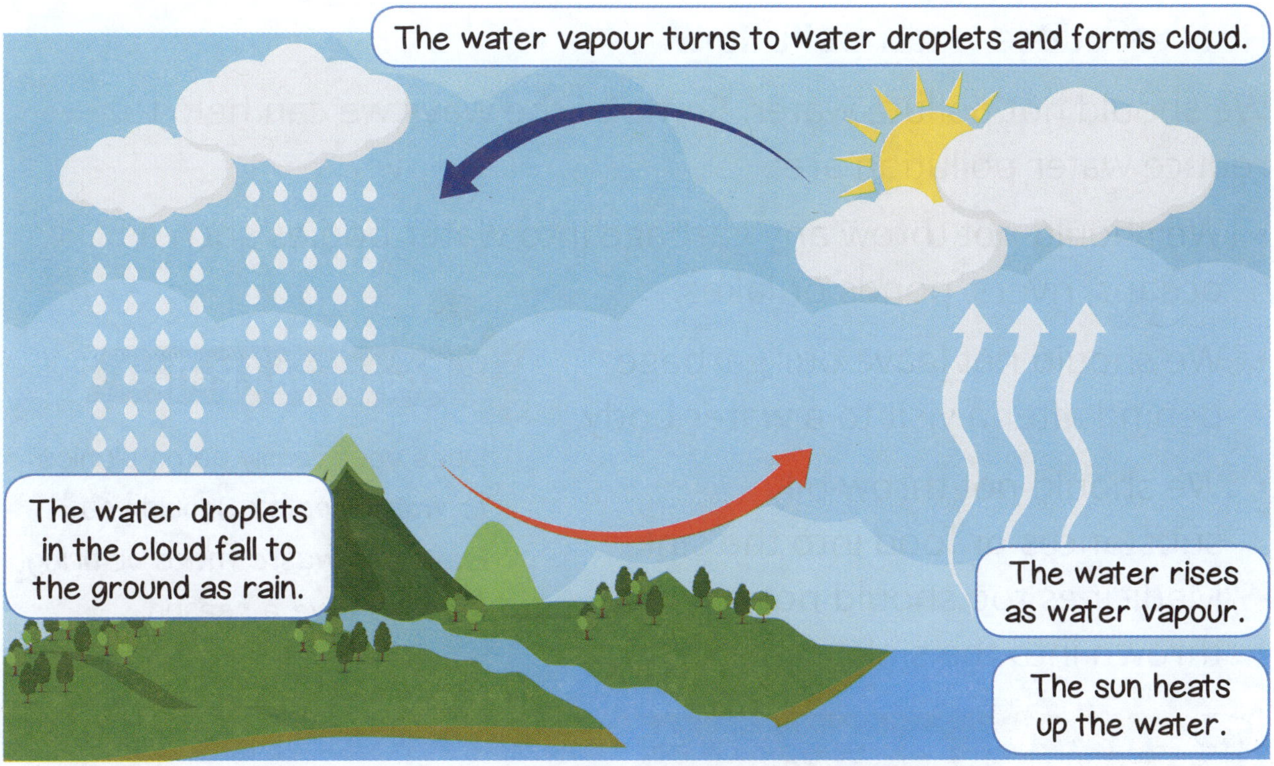

Water Cycle

Water pollution

Observe the picture. Tick (✓) how you feel.

People throw **garbage**, wastewater from their houses and factories and many other harmful things into **water bodies**. This makes the water dirty and unfit for use. This is called **water pollution**. Dirty water looks blackish and smells bad.

Effects of water pollution

Water **pollution** affects all living things.

- We will fall sick if we drink polluted water. We may suffer from diseases such as cholera and diarrhoea if we drink polluted water.
- Animals that live in water such as fish will die if the water is polluted.

How to reduce water pollution?

We should not pollute water. Some of the ways we can help to reduce water pollution are:

- We should not throw any garbage into water bodies such as oceans, rivers, ponds or lakes.
- We should not leave our garbage behind after a visit to a water body.
- We should not throw oily substances or food into the sink. Medicines too should not be thrown into the sink.

Engage and Reflect

Does your family go on picnics to water spots? Should you leave the waste there or bring it back? Give a reason.

Clean drinking water

The water we get from the taps may not be safe for drinking. We need to purify the water before drinking.

How can we make our water clean and safe for drinking?

Boiling is one of the ways to make water fit for drinking. It kills the germs present in the water. Using **water filter** also gives us clean water for drinking.

Picture Box

Tick (✓) the good practice and cross (✗) the bad practice.

i. 

ii. 

iii. 

Points to Remember

- Some of the sources of water are rain, underground water, rivers, seas and oceans.
- Water exists in three forms—solid, liquid and gas.
- The continuous movement of water from land into the air and back to the land is called the 'water cycle'.
- The dirtying of water by harmful things is called water pollution.
- Dirty water is harmful for all living things.
- Boiling and using water filter are two ways of making water fit for drinking.

Vocabulary

vapour: steam

garbage: waste

water bodies: river, sea, ocean, lake, etc.

snow: small white pieces of water that fall from the sky when it is very cold

hail: chunks of ice falling from the sky

pollution: presence of harmful substances

filter: something that removes dirty particles from water

purify: to remove dirty particles

Exercises

I. Objective Questions

1. Tick (✓) the correct answer.

i. Which of the following is not part of the water cycle?

a. Water changes to water vapour

b. Water is filtered

c. Water vapour changes to water droplets

d. Water droplets fall as rain

ii. Which is the odd one out?

a. Ice b. Snow c. Hail d. Water vapour

iii. What does water pollution mean?

a. To make water clean
b. To boil water
c. To filter water
d. To make water dirty

iv. Gaurav spilled water in his balcony while watering the plants. After a while, Gaurav found that there was no more spilled water. What happened to the water?

a. The water has changed to water vapour.
b. The water has changed to water droplets.
c. The water had fallen off the balcony.
d. All of the above.

v. How can water be made fit for drinking?

a. By boiling
b. By storing
c. By cooling
d. By stirring it with a spoon

2. Fill in the blanks by choosing the words given in the box.

rain	waste	ill	clouds	water vapour

i. Drinking dirty water makes us ________________.

ii. Throwing ________________ into water bodies causes water pollution.

iii. Heat from the sun changes water into ________________.

iv. Water as ________________ falls back on land from clouds.

v. Water vapours rise up and cool down forming ________________.

3. Write T for True and F for False.

i. Only river water evaporates during the water cycle. ☐

ii. Water exists in only one form. ☐

iii. Tap water is cleaner than boiled water. ☐

iv. We should throw garbage into water bodies. ☐

v. Dirty water smells bad. ☐

II. Subjective Question

1. How does the water around us become dirty?

____

____

2. What will happen if we drink dirty water?

____

____

3. Write two ways to obtain clean drinking water.

____

____

4. What happens after the water vapour is high up in the sky?

____

____

III. HOTS

1. Sarita kept two containers filled with water near her window. She covered one container and left the other one uncovered. In which container will the water level decrease first?

____

____

2. When a glass of cold water is placed outside, you will observe water droplets on the surface of the glass. Did the water droplets come from inside the glass or from the surroundings?

[Hint: Remember water evaporates when left in any container; where does it go?]

____

____

____

21st Century Skills | Life skills and values

Heena was watching the rain through her window. She noticed that a lot of rainwater flowed into the drain.

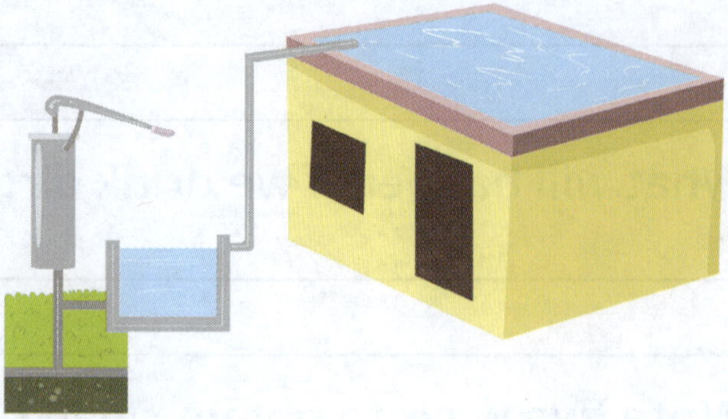

She went to her mother and asked, "Mom, there is so much water around us. Why do you still ask me to use less water? Can we not use this rainwater for our daily needs?"

"It's a good thought Heena. We can save this rainwater", said the mother. They started collecting and storing the rainwater in a tank. They used this water for cleaning and watering their plants.

Save and use rainwater.

Creators Corner

Make a model of the water cycle. Use cotton to form the clouds, yellow coloured paper for the sun, blue buttons for rain and green coloured paper for the trees.

Cross Connect (Writing)

Are there any water bodies around you? What is it? Write five sentences about it.

____

____

____

Try It

Do this activity with the help of your teacher an adult.

1. Place some ice cubes in a container that can be heated.
2. Place the container over a stove.

   The ice cubes will slowly melt and change into water. After a while, the water will start changing into water vapour. You will be able to see the water vapour rise in the container.
3. Place a lid over the container. Take it off the stove.
4. Remove the lid. The water vapour will rise and change into water droplets. These will be formed on the lid.
5. Put the water back into the freezer for it to change into ice!

This activity shows that water can be changed from one form to another by heating or cooling.

8

The Earth

Curricular Goals	Competencies
CG-6 Children develop a positive regard for the natural environment around them	C-6.1 Shows care for and joy in engaging with all life forms
CG-7 Children make sense of world around through observation and logical thinking	C-7.2 Observes and understands cause and effect relationships in nature by forming simple hypothesis and uses observations to explain their hypothesis

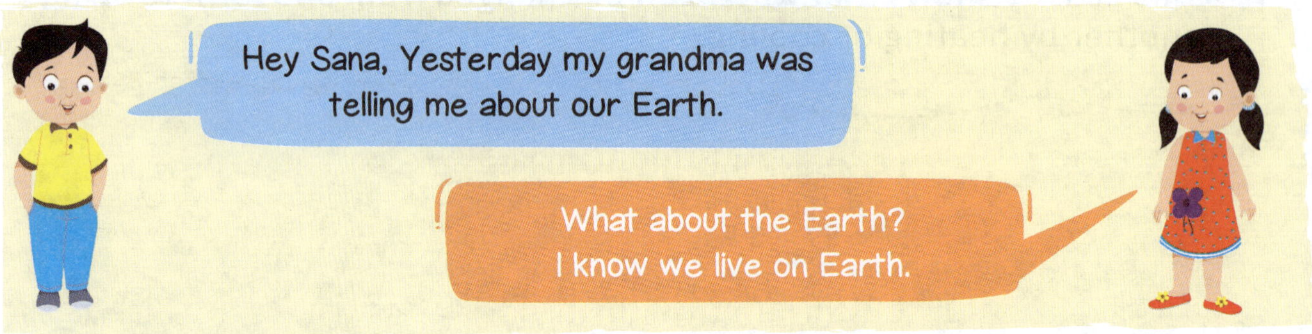

Let's Start

Cotton-bud painting

Using cotton buds, paint the picture by matching the letter with the colour as given below.

O – Orange colour
G – Green colour
B – Blue colour

Let us learn about Earth and its landforms.

We live on Earth. It is our home. The Earth is round and looks like a huge ball.

The Earth is made up of land and water. It is also called a **blue planet** as it has more water than land. It also has air.

Landforms

The land on the Earth is not the same everywhere. It has different land forms. A **landform** is a **natural** feature on the Earth's surface.

Mountain

Each landform has different features. Landforms affect the weather, climate and **lifestyle** of the people living there.

A **mountain** is a high raised land on Earth. Mountains have steep, rough sides. The pointed tip, at the top, is called the peak. Some mountain peaks are covered with snow. The famous mountain peaks of India are Kanchenjunga and Nanda Devi.

Hill

A **hill** is a raised part of the land that is higher than its surrounding areas. Hills are lower than the mountains. Towns located on the hills are called hill stations. Ooty and Manali are famous hill stations of India.

Plateau

A **plateau** is a raised part of the land. It is flat on top with very steep on the sides. The **steep** sides of plateaus are called cliffs.

The Deccan Plateau is the largest plateau in India.

A **valley** is a low-lying area of land between two hills or mountains. Kashmir Valley, Chenab Valley and Kangra Valley are some of the well-known valleys of India.

Valley

A plain is a wide, flat area of land. Many small and big cities are located on the plains. People grow crops on the plains.

Fact Check

The world's highest mountain on land is Mount Everest.

Resources

Resources are the necessary materials that we need to live. We get these resources from nature. These are called natural resources.

The Earth's natural resources include air, water, soil, plants and animals, coal and oil.

Some of the natural resources that we need in our daily lives are food, air and water. Other resources like buildings, tables, chairs, television sets, etc., are made by people to make our lives better.

Do you know what chairs are made of?

We plant a seed.

It grows into a tree.

We get wood from trees.

We make furniture, such as a chair, table and bed, from wood.

Importance of natural resources

We cannot live without natural resources. We need air to breathe, water to drink, wood to built homes and furniture. We need coal and oil to heat our homes and power our cars. We get coal and oil from deep within the Earth's surface.

Trees, plants and animals are important natural resources. We cannot live without these natural resources.

Recall some of their uses and discuss in class.

Plants grow on land and in water. On land, plants grow in soil. Soil is home to many animals and insects.

There are natural resources deep within the Earth such as coal and oil. These help make our lives better. Do you know what they are used for?

Different yet Alike!

There are many kinds of soil. The colour of soil is different in different places on Earth.

Engage and Reflect

Why is it important to take care of the Earth's resources?

Coal is used in industries for burning. Oil is used to make petrol, diesel and cooking gas. Petrol and diesel are used in vehicles such as cars, buses, and trucks.

We should care for our natural resources. Some resources like oil and coal take many years to form. We should do our part to protect the Earth and use its resources carefully.

Picture Box

Tick (✓) the good practice and cross (✗) the bad practice.

i.  ☐

ii.  ☐

iii.  ☐

Points to Remember

- We live on the Earth.
- The Earth is covered by land and water.
- A mountain is a high raised land on Earth.
- A hill is a raised raised part of the land that is higher than its surrounding areas.
- A valley is a low-lying area of land between hills or mountains.
- A plateau is a highland which is flat on top with steep sides.
- A plain is a wide, flat piece of land.
- The Earth's natural resources include air, water, soil, plants, animals, coal and oil.
- We should care for our natural resources. They take many years to form.

Vocabulary

landform: a natural feature on the Earth

lifestyle: the way we live

natural: available in nature; not made by humans

steep: sharp slope

rise: move from lower to higher

resource: things we need every day to live

Exercises

I. Objective Questions

1. Tick (✓) the correct answer.

i. What are landforms?

a. Parks and play grounds on land
b. Houses and buildings on land
c. Natural formation of dirt and rocks
d. Resources on land

ii. Which of the following is a plain?

a. 
b. 
c. 
d. 

iii. Which of the following describes a valley?

a. A flat high land

b. A low land lying between mountains or hills

c. A high land with a peak

d. A raised land with a rounded top

iv. Which of the following are Earth's natural resources?

a. Water b. Oil c. Coal d. All of the above

v. Which of the following is not a natural resource?

a. Petrol b. Soil c. Plants d. Television set

2. Fill in the blanks using the words from the box.

Coal	plains	peak	cliffs	lifestyle

i. Cities and towns are mostly located in the__________.

ii. Landforms affect the__________ of the people.

iii. __________ is a natural resource.

iv. The highest point on a mountain is called the __________.

v. The steep rock faces of plateaus are called __________.

3. Write T for True and F for False.

i. Hills are the highest landforms on Earth. ☐

ii. Our Earth has more land than water. ☐

iii. Oil and coal are made by people. ☐

iv. A wooden table is a natural resource as it is made of wood. ☐

v. Natural resources should be used wisely. ☐

II. Subjective Questions

1. Why are plains the most suitable landforms to live in?

____

2. What is a plateau?

____

3. What is a valley?

____

4. What are natural resources? Name five natural resources we get from Earth.

____

III. HOTS

1. Identify the type of land form you live on. Give a reason.

____

2. Find the following words in the word-search.

Landform	Mountain	Resource	Earth
Valley	Plain	Hill	Peak

Z	H	Y	K	Y	Q	L	Q	L	Q
L	I	G	T	J	L	U	E	J	J
A	L	X	V	A	L	L	E	Y	R
N	L	P	L	A	I	N	P	D	E
D	M	O	U	N	T	A	I	N	S
F	P	L	A	T	E	A	U	G	O
O	P	C	L	I	F	F	S	F	U
R	E	V	F	H	P	Z	Q	L	R
M	A	F	E	A	R	T	H	D	C
M	K	B	Y	R	P	V	A	X	E

21st Century Skills
Life skills and values

Jasmine was very happy. She celebrated Earth Day in school. The Earth day is celebrated every year on April 22.

They planted saplings. They participated in a painting competition that was organised. They saw a short film about the Earth Day.

They learnt about how the Earth provides us with so many important resources. It is our job to be kind towards it and protect it.

It is important to take care of the Earth.

Creators Corner

Collect pictures and make a poster on the topic 'Save Earth'.

Cross Connect (Writing)

Imagine the Earth was flat. It did not have other landforms. List three things that we will not be able to do.

____

____

____

____

Try It

Along with your teacher, walk around the school in pairs and make a list of the natural resources around you.

9 The Sky

Curricular Goals	Competencies
CG-6 Children develop a positive regard for the natural environment around them	C-6.1 Shows care for and joy in engaging with all life forms
CG-7 Children make sense of world around through observation and logical thinking	C-7.2 Observes and understands cause and effect relationships in nature by forming simple hypothesis and uses observations to explain their hypothesis

Let's Start

Paint your stars!

Take a shoe box, black watercolour, a paintbrush and wax candles.

Draw small stars and the Moon using the wax candles on the shoe box. Now, with the paintbrush, colour the whole shoe box with the black watercolour.

Magic! Your stars start shining.

Let us learn about the sky

When we wakeup in the morning, it is bright outside. We see the Sun in the sky during the daytime.

Day

At night, we cannot see the Sun. It is dark. We see the Moon and stars twinkling in the sky.

Night

The Sun

We see the Sun during the day. It gives us heat and light. All living things need sunlight to live.

The Sun rises in the east and sets in the west. The position of the Sun changes throughout the day. In the morning, we see it rise in the east. At noon, it shines brightly and is right overhead. In the evening, it sets in the west. The time when the Sun rises is called sunrise and the time when it sets is called sunset.

The Sun is a big ball of fire.

The Moon

We see the Moon at night. Sometimes we can see it during the day. The Moon is a big round ball. It is much smaller than the Sun and the Earth. It is nearer to the Earth than the Sun. The Moon moves around the Earth.

Phases of the Moon

The Moon is round in shape. However, the shape of the Moon changes every night.

- When the Moon is round it is the **Full Moon.**
- When the Moon is arc-shaped, it is the **Crescent Moon.**
- When the moon is half circle, it is the **Half Moon.**
- When we do not see the moon, it is the **New Moon.**

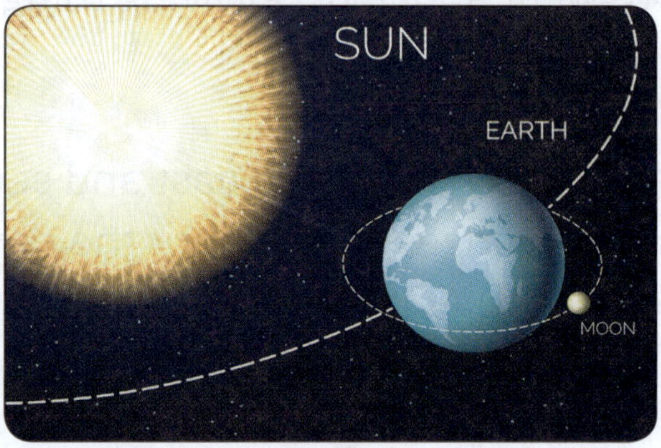

The Sun, Earth and Moon

Engage and Reflect

Do you think we can live on the Moon? Why or why not?

The different shapes of the Moon that we see at different times of the month are called the **phases** of the Moon.

Star

We see many stars **twinkling** in the sky on a clear night. They look **tiny** as they are very far away from us. We cannot see the stars during the daytime because of the bright light of the Sun.

Twinkling stars on a clear night

Many people enjoy watching the night sky and looking at the Moon and the stars through binoculars or telescopes.

A parent and child looking up at the stars

Different yet Alike!

The Moon shines brightly in the night sky. This light that we see does not come from the Moon. It is actually the light from the Sun. The Moon shines because its surface reflects light from the Sun.

Fact Check

Scientists have made rockets that can take humans to the moon. Neil Armstrong was the first man to step on the moon on July 20, 1969.

Picture Box

Tick (✓) the good practice and cross (✗) the bad practice.

i.  ☐

ii.  ☐

iii.  ☐

Points to Remember

- The Sun is a big ball of fire.
- The Sun gives us heat and light.
- The Moon is a big round ball.
- The different shapes of the Moon are called the phases of the Moon.
- Stars look tiny as they are very far away from us.

Vocabulary

phases: different stages

tiny: very small

twinkling: shining light that dims and brightens

Exercises

I. Objective Questions

1. Tick (✓) the correct answer.

i. Which of the following is not seen in the sky during the day?

a. 

b. 

c. 

d. 

ii. Which of the following gives us both heat and light?

a. the Moon b. the Sun c. the Stars d. the Earth

iii. Which is the correct order in terms of size, from the smallest to the biggest?

a. Sun Earth Moon b. Moon Earth Sun

c. Earth Moon Sun d. Sun Moon Earth

iv. Which of the following is not correct?

a. The Sun gives us heat.

b. The plants make food with the help of sunlight.

c. The animals do not need the Sun.

d. The Sun sets in the west.

v. Which of the following is used for watching the stars at night?

a. Sunglasses b. Mirror c. Telescope d. Television

2. Fill in the blanks using the words from the box.

phases	sky	Earth	stars	fire

i. The Sun is a big ball of __________.

ii. The Moon moves around the __________.

iii. We can see Stars, the Sun and the Moon in the __________.

iv. The different shapes of the Moon that we see from the Earth are called the Moon's __________.

v. __________ look tiny as they are far away from the Earth.

3. Write T for True and F for False.

i. We should look directly at the Sun. ☐

ii. The Earth goes around the moon. ☐

iii. The Moon is a big ball of fire. ☐

iv. The Sun gives us heat to dry our clothes. ☐

v. The Sun sets in the East. ☐

II. Subjective Questions

1. Describe the Sun.

2. Draw the different phases of the Moon and name them.

3. Why to the stars look small ?

4. Why cannot we see stars during the daytime?

III. HOTS

1. Ganesh observed the Half-Moon in the clear sky on Monday night. The next night, it was cloudy. His sister said it was a New Moon day. Ganesh said it wasn't. Who is correct? Explain.

2. We can see more stars in the sky in the villages than in the cities. Why?

21st Century Skills — Life skills and values

Keshav had learnt in school that the Sun's heat can be used in many ways.

He was delighted when his family decided to set up solar panels on their roof. He was amazed to see that these solar panels helped in producing electricity and in heating water. He was very excited to see his television and fan running on such electricity.

We should also use solar energy and save electricity.

Creators Corner

Take a chart paper. Draw a line in the middle. On one side, make a drawing of the sky during the day. On the other side, make a picture of the sky during the night. You can even collect and paste pictures of the Sun, the Moon and stars.

Cross Connect (Writing)

Look at the pictures. Write a few sentences about what you feel when you see these objects.

Try It

Go out for a walk at night with your family. Observe the stars and Moon. Share your experience.

10 Clothes We Wear

Curricular Goals	Competencies
CG-7 Children make sense of world around through observation and logical thinking	C-7.1 Observes and understands different categories of objects and relationships between them C-7.2 Observes and understands cause and effect relationships in nature by forming simple hypothesis and uses observations to explain their hypothesis

Let's Start

Decorate the dress!

Decorate the dress of your choice using colours, stars, glitters, sparkles, etc.

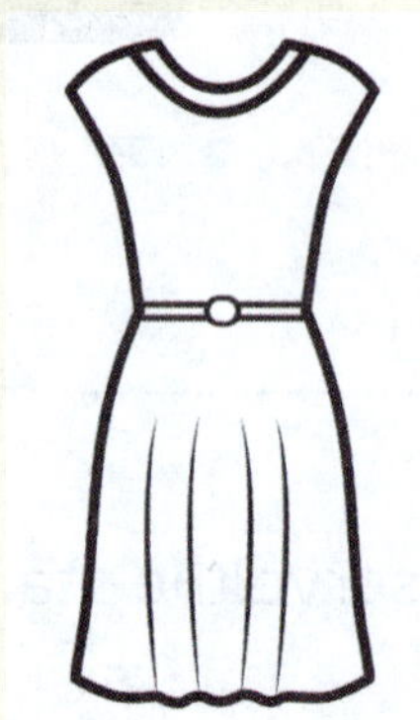

Let us learn about the clothes we wear.

We need clothes to protect us from heat, cold, dust and rain.

People wear clothes according to their age, tradition, place, season or the work they do.

Clothes according to seasons

Summer season

If it is very hot, people wear light coloured and loose clothes. People wear cotton clothes in summer. Cotton clothes keep our body cool. It **absorbs** the sweat.

Fact Check

Early humans wore clothes made of grass, leaves and animal skin.

Rainy season

What do you wear when you have to go out on a rainy day?

On a rainy day, we wear waterproof clothes. We wear raincoats and gumboots to keep ourselves dry in the rain.

Winter season

We wear clothes that keep our bodies warm in the winter season. Clothes made of wool, like sweaters, jackets, caps, shawls,etc., are worn in winters.

Clothes according to tradition

People in different parts of our country wear different types of clothes. They are called traditional dresses.

West Bengal

Kerala

Gujarat

Assam

Punjab

Ladakh

Traditional dresses from different states of India

People living in other countries too have their own traditional dresses.

China

Bhutan

Japan

Italy

Saudi Arabia

Traditional dresses worn by people in different countries

Special clothes for special jobs

- In a school, all students wear the same type of dress. People who do special kinds of jobs also wear **special** clothes to work. This special set of clothes is called a uniform.

Students in their school uniform

Adults also wear uniforms.

Engage and Reflect

Will you like if schools did not ask you to wear uniforms? Why?

Can you identify and name the special jobs people do just by looking at their clothes? Let us name these jobs.

Policeofficer

Postman

Doctor

Solider

Astronaut

Lawyer

Firefighter

Nurse

What are clothes made of and how are they made?

We get cotton from the cotton plant. This cotton is made into threads. These threads are then made into cloth using some special machines called looms.

Cotton plant

Cotton thread

Weaving of cloth

Cotton cloth

We get wool from sheep. The wool is cleaned, washed and dried. It is then made into woollen threads. These threads are used for making woollen clothes.

Sheep

Yarn

Woollen clothes

We get silk from the cocoon of the silkworm. The silk obtained from the cocoon is made into threads. These threads are made into cloth.

Silkworm

Cocoon

Silk thread

Silk cloth

Taking care of clothes

We should take care of our clothes just as we take care of our body. Some ways in which we can take care of our clothes are:

- Wash them with clean water and soap
- Dry them properly
- Iron them carefully
- Keep them at proper place

Different yet Alike!

Hats and caps are also a part of our dresses. There are many different types of hats and caps.

Which is your favourite?

Picture Box

Tick (✓) the good practice and cross (✗) the bad practice.

i.  ☐

ii.  ☐

iii.  ☐

Points to Remember

- We need clothes to protect us from the heat, cold, dust and rain.
- Cotton clothes are worn in summer.
- We wear raincoats and gumboots on rainy days.
- We wear woollen clothes in winter.
- Students wear a uniform to school. People who do special jobs like police officers, doctors, nurses and firefighters also wear a uniform.
- We should wear clean clothes. We should care for our clothes.

Vocabulary

absorbing: take in or soak up

waterproof: that does not get wet when water falls on it

tradition: habits that are followed by a group of people

special: particular

identify: find out

Exercises

I. Objective Questions

1. Tick (✓) the correct answer.

i. What is the dress that we wear to school called?

a. Party wear
b. Traditional dress
c. Uniform
d. Woollen dress

ii. Identify the INCORRECT sentence from the following.

a. The clothes we wear differ from one place to another.
b. Depending on the season, the dressing style also changes.
c. Different professions can be identified from the clothes.
d. We wear uniforms for special occasions.

iii. Which of the following do we get from sheep?

a. wool b. cotton c. cocoon d. silk

iv. It is cold outside, and you want to go out to play. Your mother wants you to wear _____before you go out.

a. Shirt b. Pants c. Sweater d. Belt

v. Which of the following is not used on a sunny day?

a. cap b. raincoat c. handkerchief d. t-shirt

2. Fill in the blanks using the words given in the box.

waterproof	traditional	woollen	silkworm	clothes

i. During winter, we prefer to wear _______________ clothes.

ii. We can identify doctors by looking at their _______________.

iii. People usually wear _______________ dresses during festivals.

iv. The clothes we wear to go out in the rain are made of _______________ cloth.

v. We get silk from the _______________.

3. Write T for True and F for False.

i. Different states of India have their traditional dresses. ☐

ii. Loose and light-coloured clothes are preferred during winters. ☐

iii. We can identify a soldier by looking at his clothes. ☐

iv. We should wear the same t-shirt for three to four days continuously without washing it. ☐

v. We get wool from plants. ☐

II. Subjective Questions

1. Why do we wear clothes?

2. What should we wear in the rainy season to avoid getting wet in the rain?

3. From what do we get silk cloth?

4. How should we take care of our clothes?

III. HOTS

1. Ooty (Udhagamandalam) is a very cold place in south India. If you plan a trip to Ooty, what kind of clothes would you pack?

2. Help Jasmine select clothes for different occasions. Write on the blanks.

Occasion	Clothes
Hot summer day	Silk frock
Going out in the rain	Jacket and woollen cap
On her birthday	Raincoat
On a trip to a hill station	Cotton t-shirt

21st Century Skills | Life skills and values

Every year before the beginning of winter, Senthil and his family visit an orphanage. This year, Senthil's family bought-blankets for the kids living there. Senthil has taken out some of his old clothes to be given away to the children at the orphanage. Clothes are a basic necessity. We should help the people in need by sharing clothes.

Share clothes with people in need.

Creators Corner

Collect and paste pieces of cotton, silk and woollen cloth. Also, write down which season or occasion we wear clothes that are made using these types of cloth.

Cross Connect (Writing)

Write about your favourite dress.

____

____

____

____

Try It

Let us make a bag using an old t-shirt. (Do this activity under the supervision of your teacher or an adult.)

a. Take an old t-shirt. Cut-out its sleeves and neck as shown below.

1

2

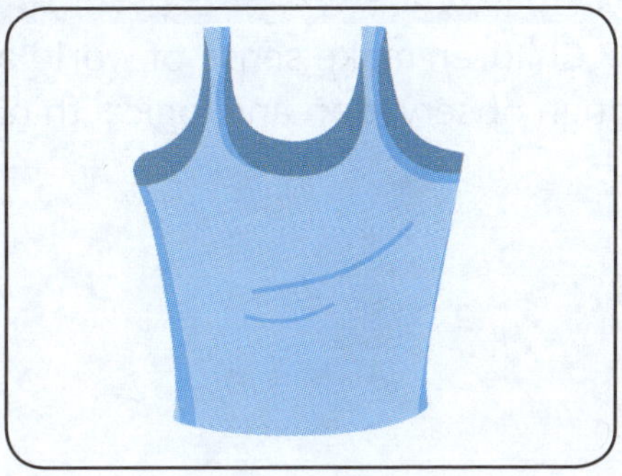

b. Turn the t-shirt inside out. Take a thread and tie it tightly at the bottom.

3

c. Turn the right side of the t-shirt out. Your bag is ready for use!

4

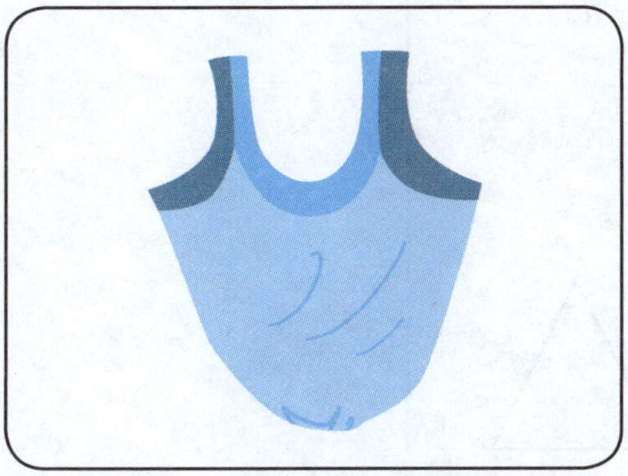

11 Houses

Curricular Goals	Competencies
CG-7 Children make sense of world around through observation and logical thinking	C-7.1 Observes and understands different categories of objects and relationships between them C-7.2 Observes and understands cause and effect relationships in nature by forming simple hypothesis and uses observations to explain their hypothesis

Let's Start

Make a House with Shapes!

Draw a house using these shapes:

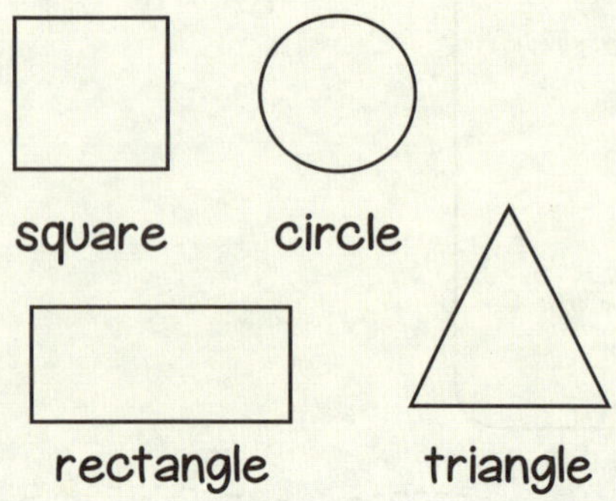

Let us read about houses.

We live in a house. A house provides us shelter and safety. It protects us from heat, cold, rain, thieves, wild animals, dirt and dust.

A house can be big or small.
A house has a roof and walls.
It also has many rooms with doors and windows.

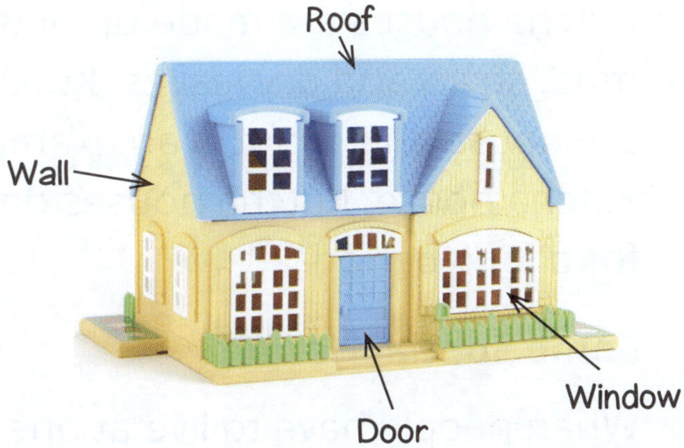

Different kinds of houses

There are different types of houses built in different places. They are pucca houses, kutcha houses and temporary houses. We use different types of materials to build houses.

Pucca House

Pucca houses are made of bricks, cement, iron rods and steel. Pucca houses are strong. These are also called permanent houses.

A pucca house can be a single-store house or a multi-storey building. A few examples of pucca houses are flats, mansions and bungalows.

Flats

Bungalow

Kutcha House

Kutcha house

Kutcha houses are made up of wood, mud, straw and dry leaves. Kutcha houses are not strong. A hut is an example of a kutcha house. Kutcha houses do not last for a long period.

Some Special Houses

When people have to live at one place for a very short time, they build houses which are not fixed and can be moved easily from one place to another. Such houses are called **temporary houses.** The different types of temporary houses are given below:

A modern caravan

- A **Caravan** is a house on wheels. It can be moved from one place to another easily. People who enjoy travelling use caravans that are built in big vehicles. They have all of the comforts of home and are also called a mobile homes.

Tent

- A **tent** is a house made of a special cloth. It is used by soldiers when they have to move from one place to another. Some tourists and travellers also live in tents while travelling.

A houseboat

- A **houseboat is** a house that is built on a boat. It is a floating house. In India, houseboats are found in Kashmir and Kerala. Houseboats have all the comforts of a house.

- An **Igloo or** a snow house is made of snow or **blocks** of snow. People living in very cold places make igloos to protect themselves from the cold. Although igloos are made of snow, they are warm from inside.

An igloo

Different yet Alike!

Houses have different kinds of roofs.

Caring for our house

We should keep our house clean and tidy. We can care for our house by doing the following:

- Open windows and doors to let the sunlight and fresh air into the house.
- Place in-door plants to purify the air inside the house.
- Make your bed each morning.
- Dust your table and arrange your things properly.
- A wire mesh on the doors and windows helps to avoid mosquitoes and other insects in the house.

Fact Check

A tree house is a house that is built on a tree trunk above the ground. It is made of wood, bamboo and leaves. Tree houses are used for tourism purposes and as observation stations.

Picture Box

Tick (✓) the good practice and cross (✗) the bad practice.

i. 

ii. 

iii. 

Engage and Reflect

Which of the following describes your room?

- Always neat and clean and everything in its proper place.
- Usually neat and clean, and some things out of their place.
- Always messy with things spread all around.

Points to Remember

- We need a house for shelter and safety.
- A house protects us from heat, cold, rain, thieves, wild animals, dirt and dust.
- Pucca houses are strong and long lasting. They are made of brick, cement and iron rods.
- Kutcha houses are made of mud, grass and leaves.
- Temporary houses can be moved from one place to another.
- Caravan, tent, igloo and houseboats are examples of temporary houses.
- A caravan is a house on wheels.
- A tent is a house made of special kind of cloth.
- An igloo is made of blocks of snow.
- We should keep our house clean.

Vocabulary

temporary: only for some time

permanent: lasting for a long time

straw: dried stem of grain

blocks: big pieces

Exercises

I. Objective Questions

1. Tick (✓) the correct answer.

i. Which of the following is correct about a pucca house?

a. It is built for temporary use.

b. It is made from wood, straw and dry leaves.

c. It can be blown away by strong winds.

d. It is made from iron, steel, cement and bricks.

ii. Choose the correct order of houses starting with the least strong to the strongest.

a. Hut Tent Bungalow b. Tent Hut Bungalow

c. Bungalow Tent Hut d. Hut Bungalow Tent

iii. Identify the house made of snow.

a.  b.  c.  d. 

iv. Ritesh went to Ladakh on a trip. He stayed in a tent for a night. What kind of house is a tent?

a. Pucca house b. Temporary house

c. Kutcha house d. Permanent house

v. How often should we clean our house?

a. daily

b. weekly

c. monthly

d. every fortnight

2. Fill in the blanks using the words given in the box.

tents	caravan	house	floating	pucca

i. We need a__________ to live in.

ii. The house on wheels is called a __________.

iii. People who go camping may live in __________.

iv. __________ houses are strong and long lasting.

v. Houseboat is a __________ house.

3. Write T for True and F for False.

i. A house protects us only from heat. ☐

ii. A kutcha house is not strong. ☐

iii. A flat and a bungalow mean the same. ☐

iv. A houseboat and a caravan are made of the same material. ☐

v. Temporary houses can be moved from one place to another. ☐

II. Subjective Questions

1. Why do we need a house?

____

2. What are pucca houses? What are they made of?

____

3. List the different types of special houses.

____

4. What materials are used in building temporary houses?

____

III. HOTS

1. Are there houses made of blocks of ice in India? Why?

____

____

2. Complete the crossword puzzle given below.

Across

2. Houses have this on windows to avoid mosquitoes
6. A house built on a tree trunk
7. An example of kutcha house
8. This type of house is made of bricks and cement

Down

1. House made of special cloth
3. House found in very cold regions
4. Floating House
5. House on wheels

21st Century Skills

Life skills and values

Roshan helps his parents in cleaning the house.

He keeps his study table neat and tidy. He puts away his toys after playing. He makes his bed in the mornings too.

Like Roshan, you should help your family keep the house clean.

Help your family in keeping the house clean.

Creators Corner

Make a house using ice-cream sticks on a chart paper.

Cross Connect (Writing)

Write about your dream house. The following points will help you:

- What type of house will it be?
- How many rooms will it have?
- Will there be space around the house for a garden?

____

____

Try It

Make a list of the different types of houses that you see on your way to school.

12 My Neighbourhood

Curricular Goals	Competencies
CG-4 Children develop emotional intelligence, i.e., the ability to understand and manage their own emotions, and responds positively to social norms	C-4.1 Starts recognising 'self' as an individual belonging to a family and community C-4.3 Interacts comfortably with other children and adults
CG-7 Children make sense of world around through observation and logical thinking	C-7.1 Observes and understands different categories of objects and relationships between them C-7.2 Observes and understands cause and effect relationships in nature by forming simple hypothesis and uses observations to explain their hypothesis C-7.3 Uses appropriate tools and technology in daily life situations and for learning

Let's Start

Greeting Card

Make a 'Thank You' greeting card for your neighbour.

Our Neighbourhood

Let us learn about our neighbourhood

The place where we live and its surroundings are known as our neighbourhood. There are different places in our neighbourhood that make our lives comfortable.

Neighbourhoods have different places around them

Places in our neighbourhood.

Neighbourhoods have markets, hospitals, banks and ATMs, parks and schools. Let us read about how each of these places help us.

- We go to the market to buy **groceries**, vegetables, clothes, books,
- toys, etc.
- We visit a hospital when we are not well. We go there to get **treatment**.
- We visit an ATM or a bank to **withdraw** money. In a bank, we can also **deposit** money and **borrow** money.
- We go to a park for playing, exercising or walking.
- We go to school to learn many things.

All of us may not have the same things in the neighbourhood.

Circle the places that you see in your neighbourhood.

Park

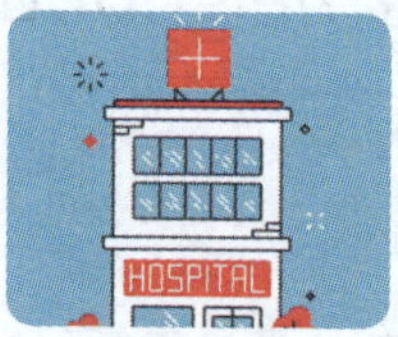

Hospital

School

ATM

Market

Engage and Reflect

What will you prefer to have in your neighbourhood: a toy shop, a park or a library? Think and answer.

Our Neighbours

The people who live around our house are our neighbours. Having a good neighbour and being a good neighbour is important.

We should treat our neighbours like good friends and help them whenever we can.

Neighbours spend time with each other. Their children play together.

Neighbours come together to celebrate **functions** and festivals.

They go out on picnics together.

Children too can learn new things from a good neighbour.

Fact Check

Early humans started to live in groups to protect themselves from animals and other dangers.

How to be a good neighbour?

Ways to be a good neighbour.

- **We must keep our neighbourhood clean.**

We should care for our neighbourhood by keeping it clean. We should throw waste trash in dustbins and not on the roads.

If we have a pet, we should not leave their waste behind. We should be a responsible neighbour and clean it.

- **We should not disturb our neighbours.**

When we listen music, we should keep the volume to a low level. Keep the doors and windows closed so that others around our house are not disturbed.

If we stay on any floor above the ground level, do not jump or play with balls inside the house. Do not do things that may disturb the families staying on the lower floors.

Do not disturb others by visiting them at **odd** times.

- **We should help our neighbours when needed.**

What would you do in the following situations?

- One day, you come home from school with your friend who is your neighbour. Both of you see a lock on the door of your friend's house.
- An old lady who lives upstairs in your building is climbing the stairs with many bags.

Many times, we come across such situations. A good neighbour always offers to help.

Engage and Reflect

Talk about your neighbours. What do you like the most about them?

- **We should respect our neighbours.**

We should greet our neighbours when we meet them.

- **We should respect our neighbour's way of living.**

Celebrate festivals together. Learn about how other communities celebrate different types of festivals.

- **We should be friendly with our neighbours.**

If you have trouble with your neighbours, talk to them and try to resolve it.

Do not have loud arguments with neighbours.

Different yet Alike!

People from several communities live in a neighbourhood. They speak different languages, follow their traditions. We can learn about different traditions when living in a community.

Picture Box

Tick (✓) the good practice and cross (×) the bad practice.

i. 

ii. 

iii. 

Points to Remember

- The place where we live and its surroundings are known as our neighbourhood.
- Some of the places in the neighbourhood are market, hospital, school and bank.
- People living around our house are our neighbours.
- We should be good to our neighbours.

Vocabulary

groceries: items of food

treatment: medical care given to sick

withdraw: to take out

deposit: to put

borrow: to take something for use and return it

function: gathering

blessing: good thing

stairs: steps

greet: to welcome someone with words or actions

resolve: to solve a problem

odd: not usual or common

climbing: to move in a way that involves going up or down

argument: to express disagreement; quarrel

Exercises

I. Objective Questions

1. Tick (✓) the correct answer.

i. Whom should we approach when there is a robbery in our neighbourhood?

a. Police b. Teacher c. Doctor d. Postman

ii. Where would you go to withdraw money?

a.  b.  c. 

d. 

iii. Mr Ramu is a singer and stays in an apartment on the third floor. He does his singing practice late at night. His neighbours have informed him that they are getting disturbed. As a good neighbour, what should he do?

a. He should give up singing.

b. He should leave the apartment.

c. He should practice during the daytime.

d. He should continue singing late at night.

iv. Which of the following is a good neighbourly behaviour?

a. Arguing with neighbour

b. Helping neighbours when they need help

c. Playing loud music

d. Dirtying the surrounding area

v. Why do we need good neighbours?

a. We feel safe when they are around us.

b. They help us whenever required.

c. We can spend good time with them.

d. All the above.

2. Fill in the blanks using the words given in the box.

festivals	greet	disturb	clean	neighbour

i. Your friend living next door is your _________.

ii. We should not _________ our neighbours.

iii. We should _________ our neighbours.

iv. We should keep our neighbourhood _________.

v. Neighbours come together to celebrate _________.

3. Write T for True and F for False.

i. We should jump and play by throwing a ball against the wall of our neighbour's house. ☐

ii. We should speak loudly while talking on a call in the park. ☐

iii. If we have any problem with our neighbour, we should talk it out with them. ☐

iv. A good neighbour offers help when needed. ☐

v. We should not celebrate festivals with our neighbours. ☐

II. Subjective Questions

1. What is a neighbourhood? Write the names of any three places in your neighbourhood.

____

2. What are the qualities of a good neighbour?

____

3. How can we help in keeping our neighbourhood clean?

____

4. Do you know all your neighbours? How often do you visit them? How do you greet them?

____

III. HOTS

1. Read the following.

Mr Rai greets his neighbours when he meets them. He speaks politely to them and asks about their well-bring.

Mr Sinha walks away without greeting his neighbours. He usually doesn't speak to any of the neighbours. Sometimes when he does speak to the neighbours, he is rude to them.

Who is a good neighbour: Mr Rai or Mr Sinha? Give a reason.

____

____

2. Your neighbour got a new pet dog and you want to play with it. What will you do?

____

____

21st Century Skills | Life skills and values

Asha is the new girl in the neighbourhood. She is feeling lonely in the new place. Abha, her neighbour, goes and greets her.

Very soon, they become good friends. When Asha's parents go out for some work, they leave Asha at Abha's house. They both love to play and have lots of fun together.

Be a welcoming neighbour!

Creators Corner

Collect photographs of five friends with their families from your neighbourhood. Paste the pictures and write their names to make an album.

Cross Connect (Writing)

Write about the person who is liked by all in your neighbourhood.

Name, Age, House or Floor no. ____________________

Why is he liked by the people? ____________________

Why do you like this person? ____________________

____

____

Try It

Ask your parents to take you for a walk around the neighbourhood. List all the things you see, hear, and smell on the way.

13 India – My Country

Curricular Goals	Competencies
CG-4 Children develop emotional intelligence, i.e., the ability to understand and manage their own emotions, and responds positively to social norms	C-4.1 Starts recognising 'self' as an individual belonging to a family and community

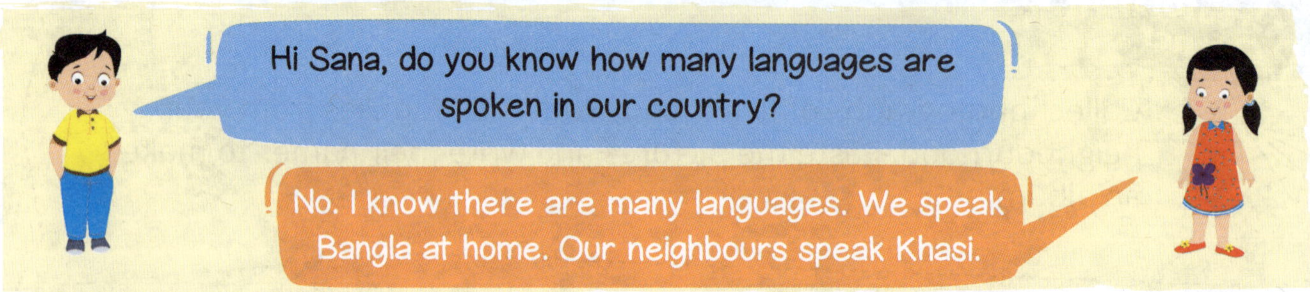

Let's Start

Finger Painting

Dip your finger tips in different poster colours. Now make fingerprints by placing your fingertips gently on the map. Now keep doing the same till you have coloured the whole map.

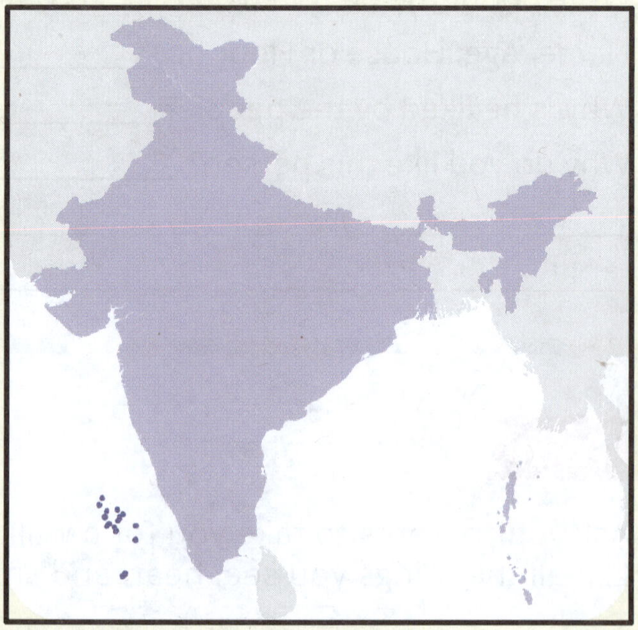

Let us learn about our country.

India is a **diverse** country in many ways. We have people of different religions and cultures living together happily.

Diversities of India

India is a big country. It is divided into 28 states and 8 union territories.

People in India wear different kinds of clothes, speak different languages and follow **traditions**.

Diversity in Language: We speak different languages

Many languages are spoken in India. There are 22 official languages in our country. The language are Assamese, Bengali, Bodo, Dogri, Gujarati, Hindi, Kannada, Kashmiri, Konkani, Maithili, Malayalam, Manipuri, Marathi, Nepali, Odia, Punjabi, Sanskrit, Santali, Sindhi, Tamil, Telugu and Urdu. Apart from the listed official languages, there are many other languages that are spoken in India.

- What language do you speak at home? ____________________
- Do you have any friend who speaks different language?
  ____
- In which language do you communicate with your friend?
  ____

Fact Check

The language we speak at home is called the mother tongue. It is the first language we learn to speak as babies.

Engage and Reflect

Explain one family tradition that your family follows.

Do you like it? Why or why not?

Diversity in Landforms: We have different landforms.

India has many landforms like mountains, plains and plateaus. Some parts of the country are extremely hot, whereas some parts are extremely cold.

There are also different types of crops that are grown in different parts of the country. This is due to the varied landforms that are present. This has resulted in different food habits.

Diversity in Food: We eat different kinds of food.

People in different parts of India have different food habits. Some of the dishes from different states of India are shown below:

Thukpa (Arunachal Pradesh)

Biryani (Telengana)

Makke ki roti (Punjab)

Dhokla (Gujarati)

Litti chokha (Bihar)

Pongal (Tamil Nadu)

Dishes for different parts of India

Diversity in Religion: People practice different religions.

In India, people follow different religions such as Buddhism, Christianity, Hinduism, Islam, Jainism and Sikhism.

Buddhism

Christianity

Hindusim

Jainism

Islam

Sikhism

Religions in India

We celebrate different festivals

India is known as the land of festivals. We celebrate many festivals in different parts of India. Some of the festivals are shown below:

Diwali

Christmas

Onam

Eid Ul-fitr

Durga pooja

Dussehra

Festivals of India

Fact Check

The Bahai temple, shaped like a lotus, in New Delhi, is one of the most visited temples of the world. People of all religions are welcomed here.

We have different dance forms

People dance to celebrate. There are many dance forms in India. These include classical, semi-classical and folk dances.

Bhangra (Punjab)

Bihu (Assam)

Garbha (Gujarat)

Kathakali (Kerala)

Kuchipudi (Andhra Pradesh)

Bharatnatyam (Tamil Nadu)

Different dance forms of India

We have different music forms.

There are different forms of music in India. Some of them are Hindustani, Carnatic, Semi-classical and Folk.

Points to Remember

- There are 22 official languages spoken in our country.
- People in different parts of India have different food habits.
- In India, people follow many religions.
- We celebrate different festivals in different parts of India.
- There are many dance forms and music forms in India.

Different yet Alike!

Unity in diversity is the Motto of Indians!

We live in harmony with one another.

Vocabulary

diverse: different
culture: way of life
extreme: difficult
tradition: practice
harmony: unity
pride: a feeling of self-respect
official: approved by the government

Exercises

I. Objective Questions

1. Tick (✓) the correct answer.

i. Which one of the following is true about India?

a. Only one language is spoken

b. People follow only one religion

c. All the states have the same traditions

d. It has 22 main languages.

ii. What makes India a diverse country?

a. It has many religions. b. It has many languages.

c. It has different food habits. d. All the above.

iii. Which of the following is not an Indian dance form?

a. Bhangra b. Bharatanatyam

c. Hip-hop d. Bihu

iv. "Dhokla" is a famous food item of which state of India?

a. Karnataka b. Gujarat

c. Uttar Pradesh d. Tamil Nadu

v. Choose the correct order starting from the least to the most in terms of numbers.

a. Number of languages in India

b. Number of states in India

c. Number of union territories in India

d. Both a and b

2. Fill in the blanks using the words given in the box.

22	festivals	diverse	religions	28

i. India is a __________ country.

ii. We have __________ states in India.

iii. India, has __________ official languages.

iv. India is called the land of__________.

v. People following different __________ live together in India.

3. Write T for True and F for False.

i. Though there is diversity in India, Indians stay united. ☐

ii. In our country, importance is not given to dance and music. ☐

iii. There is only one music form in India. ☐

iv. Bihu is a dance form of Gujarat. ☐

II. Subjective Questions

1. What makes India a diverse country?

____

2. List any five official languages of India. What is your mother tongue?

____

3. Name the different religions followed in India.

____

4. What is the reason for the diversity in the food habits among the people of India?

____

III. HOTS

1. Rita and her family will be moving from Goa to Tamil Nadu. Tamil Nadu has a very different food culture from that of Goa. Which of the following sentences show that Rita and her family have mixed with the new culture?

   i. They have learned new food habits from their neighbours and shared their food habits with them.

   ii. They have completely adopted the new food habits and forgetten their old food habits.

   iii. They follow only their old food habits.

   iv. They tell their neighbours that they do not like their food habits.

2. Unscramble the given words with the help of the clues.

   i. Way of life ERTUCUL C _ _ _ _ _ E

   ii. Friendship and unity OARMNYH H _ _ _ _ _ Y

   iii. Practices and habits TRONTIADIS T _ _ D _ _ _ _ N S

21st Century Skills — Life skills and values

Make a list of all the languages spoken by your classmates.
Which language is spoken by most of your classmates?
Learn to write your name in five different languages.
Respect all religions and cultures.

Creators Corner

Prepare a collage on "Unity in Diversity" by collecting pictures of different food items, clothes, dance forms and festivals of India.

Cross Connect (Writing)

Write a few lines about your state. What do you like the most about your state? What are the similarities you find with other states?

Try It

Collect the following information from five families in your neighbourhood.

Name of the family	State they belong	Two main festivals they celebrate
1.		
2.		
3.		
4.		
5.		

14 Modes of Communication

Curricular Goals	Competencies
CG-9 Children develop effective communication skills for day-to-day interactions in two languages	C-9.3 Converses fluently and can hold a meaningful conversation C-9.4 Understands oral instructions for a complex task and gives clear oral instructions for the same to others C-9.7 Knows and uses enough words to carry out day-to-day interactions effectively and can guess meaning of new words by using existing vocabulary

Let's Start

Drawing Numbers

The letters and the numbers on Mr. Rakesh's mobile phone keypad have vanished. Help him by drawing the keys and writing the digits and letters on them correctly.

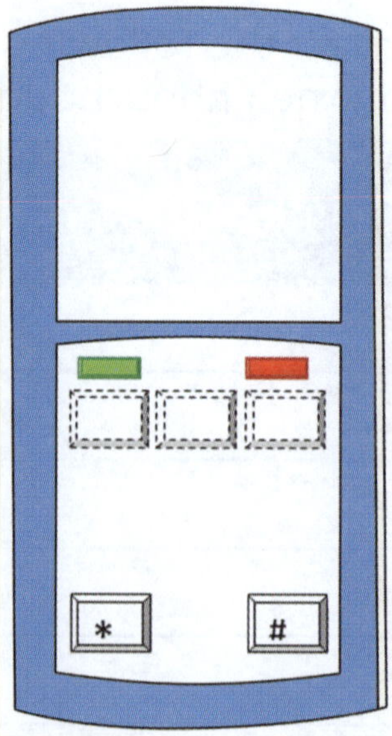

Let us learn about communication.

Every day, we talk to our parents, friends and other people about many different things. We talk to them to share ideas, thoughts, news and information. This is called **communication**. We communicate with others through speaking, writing, sign, symbol and gestures. Speaking and writing are **verbal communication**. Communication through sign, symbol and gestures are **non-verbal communication**.

Different modes of communication

We use different modes to communicate with others. Talking face to face is the simplest **mode** of communication. We also send letters, postcards, messages and talk over the phone. Let us read about them.

Letters

In earlier times, letters were given to **messengers** who would walk or ride on a horse to **deliver** them.

These days, we send letters and **parcels** to other people through post offices. Letters take a long time to reach as there are many steps involved.

- We write the letter and put it in an envelope.
- We paste a stamp and drop the envelope in a postbox.
- A postman collects the letters from the post box and takes them to the post office.
- The letters are sent to the post office in different places.
- Then, a postman delivers the letters to the given addresses.

Telephones and Mobile phones

We use telephones and mobile phones to directly talk to other people in near by or far-off places. They are the fastest modes of communication.

Messaging

Video call

The telephones that we can carry are called mobile phones. Mobile phones help us communicate with people instantly. We also use mobile phones for sending messages and video calls.

Fact Check

In earlier times, pigeons were used to deliver letters. The message was rolled and tied to the pigeon's leg.

Other modes of communication

To communicate with many people in different parts of the country or the world at the same time, we use other modes of communication, such as the radio, television or newspaper.

Radio

With the help of radio, we can send any news or message at the same time to many people. Radio is **widely** used to give information and important news about things happening in the country and the world. It is a cheaper mode of communication.

A radio

We hear a variety of programmes related to information, education and entertainment for children on radio.

Newspaper

Newspaper

A newspaper is a written form of communication. There are daily newspapers with lots of news and information in them. A newspaper has different pages for different information like the sports news, business news, children's section, world news, city news etc.

Television

Television is the most **effective** mode of communication. We can watch anything on the television.

These days, almost every home has a television. It is widely used for watching programmes on entertainment, news and sports.

Internet

Internet is another important means of communication. We use the internet for information, online shopping and educational purposes.

The internet has not only made it possible for families to talk on the mobile phone, but also to hear, write, read and see on it. We use many applications on mobile phones for this.

It is the fastest means of communication in the present times.

Emailing

Electronic mails (emails) are a way of exchanging emails or messages through telephones or computers with the help of the internet. We can send emails to people in any part of the world. To send an email, we should know the email address of the person to whom we are sending an email. An email is like a letter, but it reaches the other person much faster than the letter.

Engage and Reflect

How do you like to read your favourite story—from a storybook or on a computer screen?

Picture Box

Tick (✓) the good practice and cross (×) the bad practice.

i.

ii.

iii.

Points to Remember

- Communication is a way of sharing our messages, thoughts and information.
- The different ways of communication are reading, writing, listening, talking
or seeing.
- Talking face to face is the simplest mode of communication. Letters, telephones and mobile phones, radio, newspapers, television, and internet are the different modes of communication.
- Internet is the fastest mode of communication.

Vocabulary

mode: way

messengers: the person who carries messages

deliver: hand over something

parcel: packet

effective: helpful

widely: commonly

chat: exchange messages online

Exercises

I. Objective Questions

1. Tick (✓) the correct answer.

i. Which of the following is the slowest mode of communication?

a. 

b. 

c. 

d. 

ii. Which is the odd one out?

a. Radio   b. Telephone   c. Newspaper   d. Television

iii. Suma got hurt while playing in school. Her teacher wants to communicate this to her parents. Which mode should she use?

a. Write a letter to the parents.

b. Write an email to the parents.

c. Show her picture on the television.

d. Call her parents using a mobile phone.

iv. There may be a chance of a heavy storm in a region in the following days to come. The Government officials want to inform the people of that region. Which of the following modes of communication should they use?

a. Television

b. Radio

c. Newspapers

d. All of the above

v. Which of the following is the fastest means of communication?

a. Telephone   b. Letter   c. Radio   d. Internet

2. Fill in the blanks using the words given in the box.

communication	Internet	mobile phones
postman	telephones	

i. The exchange of information is called ______________.

ii. We use ______________ to talk to our friends staying in another city.

iii. The ______________ brings our letters and parcels.

iv. We can make video calls to our friends on ______________.

v. Through the ______________, we can chat, share pictures or videos.

3. Write **T** for True and **F** for false.

i. The telephone is a faster means of communication than email. ☐

ii. We can send an email to anyone from any part of the world. ☐

iii. We can use the radio to talk to our relatives. ☐

iv. We get weather news only in the newspapers. ☐

v. Radio is used for watching educational programmes. ☐

II. Subjective Questions

1. List different ways of communication.

____

2. List the different modes of communication.

____

3. How is a television different from a newspaper?

____

4. Why is the internet very important in today's world?

____

III. HOTS

1. **Your teacher has asked you to collect information on a topic. Name all the modes of communication that you can use.**

____

2. **Read the following. Choose the best mode of communication for each. Circle your answer.**

i. Manu wants to watch a cartoon movie.

Television / Radio/ Newspaper

ii. Sita wants to know about the health of her grandmother who lives in another city.

Mobile phone / Radio / Television

iii. The school wants to inform the parents that the next day is a school holiday.

Newspaper / Letter / Mobile phone

21st Century Skills — Life skills and values

Sirat was new to the school. She had a speech problem. She used to stammer while speaking. She was nervous about meeting her new classmates.

Sirat's classmates were patient with her and listen to her carefully Sirat started enjoying her time at school.

Be a good listener and help others communicate well!

Creators Corner

Collect and paste pictures of different mode of communication to make a collage.

Cross Connect (Writing)

Write a few lines on the means of communication you like. The one means of communication I like the most is ____________________ because ________________________________.

Try It

Make a phone using two paper cups and a thread.

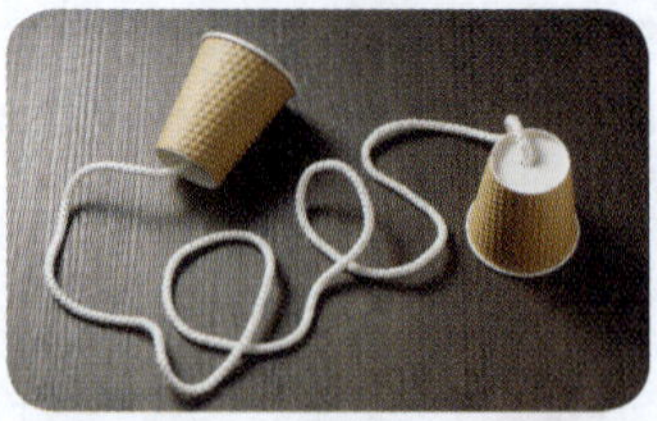

Your phone is ready. Start talking!

Take two paper cups. Make a hole on the bottom of each cup. Now take the thread and insert it into each of the holes. Tie a knot at the ends so that the thread does not come out of the paper cups when pulled.